2016

First Edition

Published and printed by

Leiston Press
Unit 1-1b Masterlord Industrial Estate,
Leiston,
Suffolk,
IP16 4JD
Tel: 01728 833003
Email: glenn@leistonpress.com
www.leistonpress.com

ISBN
978-1-911311-02-7

Preface

During Mike's final spell in hospital, while chatting with fellow patients, someone suggested that he should record his stories.

Soon after he came home, Mike started on these memoirs. They began chronologically but then seemed to veer off into particular subjects.

Unfortunately, time ran out on Mike before he could complete everything. He enjoyed relating parts of his story to his many visitors, who would often be greeted by: "Now, where did we get to last time you came?"

Although Mike was more than a little put out by the fact that his life was not going to be as long as he had hoped, through these memories he came to realise what a very full and blessed life he had lived.

This book is given with love and gratitude to all who supported us so well through Mike's final months with visits, messages, cards and phone calls but especially to those who prayed.

Please remember Mike with a smile.

God bless you all.

Thanks to Catherine and to Cheryl Payne for helping to prepare for publication.

Thankyou to Leiston Press for Printing the first edition.

Mike Rowson Memoirs of a full life

I was born at a place called Shimplingthorne, according to my birth certificate. Shimplingthorne is a building so that's what they put on my birth certificate. They have since changed it to Shimpling. On my birth certificate, obviously, is my mother, May Alberta Rowson, and my father, Howard Rowson. Catherine and I went and visited this building, so we know where I was born.

We had quite a bit of money; in fact, we had a Bentley and a Lagonda, two of the top cars. When I was growing up, somehow we appeared to be living in Bristol – heavens knows how – and my mother used to drive this Bentley, with me strapped in the seat, from Bristol to Bedford, because I do believe she worked for Harters –she was a secretary.

When my mother was growing up, Grandad was machine manager at Clays – a very good job – and they had a very nice house. They had some relations who lived at Mettingham at the Pines, who were very, very rich. They didn't have any children, so they took over mother and sent her to St Marys; I think they paid for that – St Mary's school in Bungay. She was a reasonable hockey player and then she was taken under the wing by Uncle Charlie and Aunt Nancy – they brought her up. I think they paid for her to go to a secretarial finishing school. She went from there to London and she worked in Grey's Inn – the solicitors - I think she probably was a solicitors' secretary. At the time, would you believe, we lived in the Dorchester Hotel. We appeared to have a lot of money. Father kept flipping in and out, and I vaguely remember him – not too much. Then, when we were in London I was sent to an up-market play school and I was supposed to have a godfather but he was shot down so Jon Pertwee said he would be my godfather. Going to this up-market play school, I came back with an accent, and Jon said "What on earth have you done with him, May?". I didn't see much of Jon Pertwee, but he – Worzel Gummidge – was my godfather.

Mother then decided she wanted to move nearer her parents, so got a job in Royston where she worked for Banham's solicitors. This was a normal solicitors' office, and we rented rooms at a place called Applegarth, which is a great big white place, with white railings, opposite the swimming pool at Royston. In charge of this house was a German prisoner of war who married or was partner to the person who owned the house – because up the road there was a prisoner of war camp. One of the memories I have is that someone in their wisdom bought me a great big toy wooden Lancaster plane, with propellers which went round, and for some reason I can remember a pond, which I inevitably fell in, and also I can remember this lady having a ladies' tea party. They were all in a row, sitting. In my wisdom I decided to fly this plane straight down the middle of this tea party. There was so much row – people falling off chairs…It made it to the end and of course I got a right telling off for that one.

My last memory of my father was walking from this place off to wherever.. And I never really saw him again. My mother did not want me to get in touch with him – not talk to him – and as I was duty bound to my mother – she was bringing me up - that's what I did.

And then we moved from that house – to the great North road, where we rented rooms in another big house, which was quite a nice place but unfortunately had gas lamps. And one night I discovered this gas lamp and turned it on without lighting it. Thank goodness my mother came in, or else I wouldn't be doing this now.

Anyway, mother wanted to get nearer to granny and granddad, and there was a secretarial place at Melton Constable, which was in North Norfolk – a railway junction – more about trains later. One side was an industrial town. We went to the house of Mr and Mrs Bastard who lived in Kitchener road. My mother had a job at Melton Constable Secondary School where Mr Knight was Headmaster. I went to the primary school and what my mother used to do was meet me after school and we used to go on the train to Sheringham, get off and go and have our tea and then go on the beach with a bat made by my granddad. My mother would teach me how to bat. "Play straight". And she would tell me how to bat and bowl. Hence the start of cricket. It was my mother who started it on the flat sands of Sheringham beach.

And then it was decided that the primary school should play another primary school – Barney or somewhere like that – in a game of cricket. And of course I got in the team, made a catch – but there was a very good player called Plumley and he opened the batting. I came in at number eight, and I stayed there – blocking and blocking and blocking – while he scored the runs. And I got my first mention at cricket. I remember catching a catch and as I fell down I was going to hit this puddle, so I put my hand down and technically I had made the catch but I grounded the ball, as I landed on the ball when I stopped myself from falling in the puddle. But the master of the other side said "That's Out".

Mince!

In February 1952 I was at Melton Constable Primary School, where we were always made to eat all of our lunch. This particular day it was mince. I hated mince and one of the dinner ladies said I could not go out to play until I had finished it. I was the only one left in the room. Then, the Deputy Head came in and announced that the King had died. Whereupon I said: "He must have eaten some of this mince". I was not allowed out at all!

Melton Constable was a magic town for the railways. There used to be a train that came in, went up the line and came back again. We used to hitch a ride on that. Unbelievable. Anyway, mother wanted to get nearer Bungay and there was a job at Loddon, and when she went to the interview, who should be sitting on the panel but Mr Knight from Melton Constable, who promptly said "I think Mrs Rowson would do this job very nicely". So she did.

So now we are at Loddon. I wasn't very bright. I failed the 11 plus – much to my mother's displeasure. I was very pleased I got into the As and not the Bs of the school. Anyway, somehow – I do not know how – I passed the 13 plus – two goes at 11 plus failed but somehow I passed the 13 plus to go to Wymondham College. I don't know whether my mother pulled strings or not, but when I got to Wymondham College I was bottom of the class. I couldn't do Maths, but I did manage to get General Science, Geography, History, RE – so I got about four – and my mother persuaded Mr Metcalf that I would go and try and get two more. So they persuaded me to have another year in the fifth year. It was not very nice because my friends were prefects; they could go to bed at a certain time and I still had to go to bed with the fifth year – but nevertheless, I got something else and ended up with five O-levels. My mother didn't really know what I should do but I went straight into man-service in the air force. When I applied to the air force, I was made an instrument mechanic.

When I was at Wymondham College, I played for the 2nd XI cricket team and was coached by a Welshman, Stan Montgomery, who I met later at Newport. I ran cross-country and represented Norfolk County at the Quadrangular Sports at Hewett School, Norwich, where I finished some distance behind Mike Tagg, later an Olympian runner.

I was posted from the air force recruiting office to Cardington, in Bedford. That was my first sight of the RAF. You can see the hangers from the big bypass at Bedford. And that's where I was. I then went to Bridgenorth in Shropshire. I learned more on that train journey about the facts of life than ever I would have done anywhere else. I grew up very quickly. We went to Bridgenorth, where the billets were very, very long, and anyone who was near the door had to say "NCO Present". But we discovered that one bloke could not say his r's so anytime the NCO came in he would say "NCO peasant". Well, he got moved by the authorities to a different bed.

From there, we did an eight weeks' course, and there were some funny incidents because the National Service people were on at the same time. And as we marched along, one of the National Service men saw a sixpence on the floor. He bent down to pick it up. Chaos reigned. Everyone fell over – everybody laughing – NCOs going absolutely berserk – NCO trying to get everyone in order – wonderful. He wasn't a bad footballer, the NCO, and I did play once or twice for the section – so that started on my football with the RAF.

One of the funniest things was the fog. The parade square was really, really big. Not as big as Woolwich, or, later on, Winston Churchill's funeral parade – that will come later. Anyway, this foggy morning these National Service men could not give a monkey's so we marched along – Left, Right, Left, Right, Left – and one of the back markers said "I can't see him; he's in the fog. If I can't see him, he can't see us. Let's march off the parade square to the Naafi". So we all marched off the parade square and were sat down in the Naafi getting coffee. Well, he stormed in there and sorted us all out, but we did get a description from one of the other NCOs which was really funny. He went; "Left, Right, Left Right Left – about turn – Left, Right" – petering out – he had lost us. Anyway, he could not charge all of us so he took it quite well.

In one exercise you had to get a list of things including a fish. We went by a river and said to a bloke fishing "Can we have a fish?". "Yes; OK then". So we took it to the office on the Friday and left it on the desk of the NCO. He turns up Monday morning. Imagine.

I was posted to Melksham. One of the things was half way through the training at Bridgenorth you were allowed home for the weekend. We went on a bus, travelling at about 80 miles an hour down the new M1 – no seatbelts – which now you would never do in a month of Sundays. They used to streak up and down that M1 as if they were high speed trains. Anyway, we got to London and I made my way across to Liverpool St and got home. When I got home, I obviously was in uniform, and I was polishing my buttons, and my mother said "Well, if I knew you were just going to polish buttons…" but I said I had to keep it up. Anyway, I passed out from Bridgenorth and was posted to Melksham in Wiltshire. Well as soon as I was posted to Melksham my mother said that there was a Mr Spencer. Mr Spencer apparently was Clerk of Royston, and he was Clerk of Devizes. Big man. So I used to go and stay with him in his house. I got a game of cricket for Devizes but didn't bat very much. I got a game of football for Devizes – played a bit for them but played mostly for the station. I did a year's fitters' course – managed to get through it somehow – and was posted to Cranwell.

I arrived at Cranwell and by then I was developing into a reasonable cricketer, having played for Loddon – I could bowl quite well. I then got into the Cranwell cricket team and I was captain of the Cranwell football team second eleven and very often played in the first team. I was the only non- commissioned officer in Cranwell cricket team – all the rest were officers. And there was a chap there seconded by the army called Major Thorne. Major Thorne came from Norfolk – and he played cricket for Norfolk –and after one match he said "What are you going to do while we go to the Officers' Mess" I said I would probably go to the Naafi. "Well here's some money". A pound. A pound in 1960 – thank you – a lot of money. Anyway, he was very good to me and he taught me how to swing bowl. One time we reached the final of the 20: 20 and I bowled all ten overs from one end with this fellow telling me how to swing it. I learned more in that session than ever. Wonderful man.

I played on the Orange, in front of Cranwell College, and I think the first time we probably got to the RAF cup quarter finals. Anyway, I then had to go back to Melksham for my fitters' course. And after a while I managed to pass and get through –I wasn't very good (my wife says I was dyslexic). During my time here there were two games going on at Wembley. One was England against Scotland and the other one was England against the rest of the world. So having passed out and with a few days spare I thought I would go and see if I could get into these games. No tickets but there would be. So I went down in uniform and when I got to the Scotland game I was mixed in with a load of Scots people and they shared a taxi with me, unbeknown. They were all really jolly. I got outside the ground in my uniform and there was a chap with tons of tickets. "Here you are mate, have one. I can't get rid of it now – only two minutes to go". Really, in those days, anything went. He didn't want any money for it. So I walked in, got a jolly good seat and watched England beat Scotland 9-3. 9-3; unbelievable. And I thought the best player on the ground was a chap called Baxter who played for Scotland, would you believe. But there was a goalkeeper for Scotland called Haffy – but he wasn't very happy. There was Jimmy Greaves, Bobby Robson, all the top men. So I thought – well that's good – next Saturday they play the rest of the world. So I went down again. I didn't get the same bloke but there were blokes dishing out tickets all over the place. So I walked in again, got another seat, and saw England beat the rest of the world 2-1. Fine, wonderful players – Cuscus, Gento, Yashin. I remember Yashin the goalkeeper, from Russia. Dressed all in black. Jimmy Greaves hit a shot from about thirty yards and as it sailed towards Yashin, the half time whistle went. So he punched it from about the penalty spot into the crowd. I've never seen a punch like it in all my life before. The ball was travelling like I don't know what. And he punched it into the crowd. He was fantastic. That was the best football match I have seen.

I had now qualified to go back to Cranwell. I went back to Cranwell, got in the cricket team and we got to the semi-final of the cup and we played at Clare College – unbelievable. Clare College comes later. I believe I might have got a wicket. I didn't get many runs but I was a bowler anyway. We didn't make the final but nevertheless my cricket was getting better.

Loddon Cricket Club 196?, Paul Clemence seated on left

While I was at Cranwell I worked on Jet Provosts. While I was there I then got posted to NAV squadron from the Jet Provosts, which was a great move because I could have more time to play cricket. Very often I would work nights so that I got cleared off on a Friday afternoon and I could get home. One time they were flying down to Suffolk – I don't know where –and I got a lift down with a plane and then thumbed it back up to Loddon. Very often the NAV squadron had flying classrooms to train navigators. This bloke had us landing in the North Sea – he got it wrong didn't he. Unbelievable. I was saying "I can see lights out there". I was supposed to keep my mouth shut but I couldn't really, with that. Very often, the air officer would fly his own personal Ansom, and on a particular day I was asked if I would see it off. You had to go down to the hanger, prepare it, look around it, make sure it had two wings etc. With two other guys. So I sorted this out and the AOC said "Does anyone want a trip". I shot up my hand. So off I went with the AOC who said "We can talk cricket, young Rowson". So off we went; we took off for a tour round his area – like Hemswell, Scampton, Wallington – where all the V bombers were. We got to Lincoln Cathedral. And he flew round Lincoln Cathedral. So we saw Lincoln Cathedral from the air, and we flew round there two or three times. He got to Hemswell and he said "Oh look; there's the Naafi wagon". So he reported to Hemswell that he was coming in, and they all jumped to attention, and he went off to the Officers' Mess, and I went down to the Naafi. We met again - off we went – and we got to Foldingworth. "Right, said the AOC – I am going to test your missiles". As we went above their missiles, they followed us round. My comment was "I hope they get on with you, Sir". These missiles just followed us round. That was a marvellous trip. He took me out another time – he was a lovely bloke. AOCs did come to feature prominently in my life. Cranwell was good stuff – I got time off to play cricket, time off to play football – I did do some work at some stages, would you believe, but if you played cricket and football then you were in.

Elizabeth and I were going out quite some time. She says that she ran into me in the playground! Later we were both in the choir at church and one thing led to another and we went out together. We had some good times. I remember going to the fair and Elizabeth getting her heel stuck. I used to take her to football. By that time I had bought myself a brand new mini. I saved my money up. Others were drinking and smoking but I saved my money up – and my mother did help me – and I bought myself a brand new green mini. Someone asked if I had come into an inheritance! I had one or two accidents with this mini. It was too quick for me, really, but nevertheless I had got a car. We would go backwards and forwards from Loddon to Melksham. They were building the bypass at Oxford. Well on the Friday night there was not a roundabout, but on Monday morning, at 2 o'clock in the morning, there was a roundabout. So we piled into that, looked at the mini, bounced down the other side – off we went. The other accident I had in it was when a bloke wanted a lift to town at dinner time and I shot over a corner – mud all over the road – we skidded like mad, hit this tarmacadam spraying machine and lost on points. My cap badge was bent where I had hit it. The police came along and said "Thank goodness you've done this". I thought "What?". "Yes; thank goodness you've done this – we can now charge the road people for not putting signs up. We'll take you to the garage". They were soon able to repair it and I was insured. The other time I had an accident was going too fast round a corner – I collided with a big lorry. Elizabeth had made me or bought me a thing called a "gonk". A gonk was a large sort of teddy bear thing, and it sat on the back shelf. Well, I hit the front tyre of this lorry. Obviously, the front window had gone out. I dived down. Everyone was OK except for a cut lip – we were very lucky. When we got out of the car, the lorry driver had a match in his mouth trying to light it. He was saying "Where's the baby". We were saying "What's he on about? Ah – the gonk". The gonk had flown through the front window and he thought it was a child. So we settled him down. Poor bloke – he was in a right state. He really thought it was a baby flying through the air.

So – backwards and forward to Melksham with this mini. I remember going to London once to see Chelsea play Norwich. And there was another mini in front of me. And I followed him through, rather like "The Italian Job". This bloke was loving it. He had a moustache, and a cap, and I followed him through. Every time he changed gear, I changed gear. I saw Chelsea play city – 2-0. I used to go into London to watch Norwich play. I took Elizabeth to Chelsea, on the edge of Chelsea Shed – more about that later. We sometimes went by coach from Loddon. On one particular day we went to see Sheffield United away. My friends said they would pick me up at the back gate of Cranwell. Great – OK. I had a parade that morning – but the parade was put back an hour. So the coach came from Loddon, parked outside the back gate and sounded its horn loudly whilst we were parading. "Anything to do with you, Rowson?" "No, sir – nothing to do with me". I couldn't get off parade, but in the end I got away. When I got outside, two men came past – they were looking for tickets. I had three so they took me to Sheffield United. We lost about 3-1 – big crowd. I did not know how I was going to get home. I walked along – blow me if I didn't see Ninham. Ninham was the son of a friend – I got a lift straight back home. Brilliant performance.

Another night I watched City play the Forest. We lost 1-0 and as I was driving home the dynamo packed up. I found a garage in the middle of the night. "I can fix that" said this bloke; "I enjoy fixing dynamos". So he took the dynamo out, trimmed it up, put it back – wouldn't take any money. He said "I love these cars". I got home pretty late; my mother was furious.

Memories of Winston Churchill's funeral

RAF Cranwell had a ceremonial squad for various duties such as Remembrance Sundays, funerals etc which required a guard of honour – there were about 16 people who all had to be 6ft tall. At 5ft 11¾ I was regarded as suitable. I was a bit miffed at having to do extra duties and keeping the uniform immaculate but a good thing I did!

We were told we had to do extra drill practices and provide a guard of honour for whatever dignitaries arrived at Cranwell. One of these was the Minister of Defence Denis Healey who asked a West Indian where he had come from, whereupon the reply was "Da billet, sir!"

A little later we were told about Operation Hope Not because Winston Churchill was becoming increasingly frail and we were told that if he died at a weekend we were to report straight back to Cranwell. One Sunday morning we heard the news on the radio and I had to go from Loddon to pick up a chap called James at

Covehithe and we sped off to Cranwell, parked the car and reported to the officer in charge. Collecting our best blues we boarded the bus to travel to Woolwich Barracks where the accommodation was basic.

The next morning we were on Woolwich Barracks parade square which is a massive area. I was telling a joke to our group. We were all there to be instructed in marching by the Army and coming across the square with paystick under his arm, peaked cap at a menacing angle, was a stern-looking army sergeant, marching at the double shouting: "Rowson, you do not tell jokes on my parade square!" He marched up to me while my colleagues, in fear and trepidation, said: "You've had it this time Mike" but when he reached us he said: "How are you doing Mike?" We had played cricket together somewhere!

The next day was spent marching on the square, with our own officer in charge. We were marching towards an archway – me in the front row – when coming through the archway five abreast were the Royal Marines in their white helmets and greatcoats. I thought: 'Somebody, somewhere, give an order!' Our officer, since we were such a small squad, gave the order: "Cranwell contingent disintegrate." We did and the Marines marched straight through. Unfortunately, coming round the corner on his bike was an army post boy, whistling along to the tune of Goodbye Dolly Grey. He promptly collided with the Royal Marines, who marched over him and his bike! A rather unfortunate incident.

That night we decided to go to Earl's Court to see the racing car show because I wanted to see Paddy Hopkirk's Mini which had won the Monte Carlo Rally.

The next day we had to be up, have an early breakfast and at 4a.m., having practiced reverse arms, we marched to our given positions along the funeral route. We were quite near St. Paul's. The order was given to reverse arms – which of course we did, only to find that it wasn't the official vehicle coming through but an early morning dustcart. We did similar practices for three mornings.

The day of the funeral itself was very cold and we marched to our positions at about 6 a.m. and stood in front of the crowd. When the gun carriage came through we had to reverse arms. Paddy, across the road, was too busy watching what was going on until a policeman asked if he wasn't supposed to be doing what everyone else was doing.

I was fortunate to be standing opposite an electrical shop with a TV in the window and so could keep up with what was going on. Once the coffin had been taken into St Paul's the sailors with the gun carriage stood and waited opposite us.

We marched back to our bus and returned to Cranwell once the funeral was over everyone dismissed.

Years later I gave a talk to Reepham WI about my time in the RAF and included the above story. One of the ladies went home and must have talked to her husband about it and it turned out he was one of the sailors pulling the gun carriage.

Another incident from about this time, one of the duties of Cranwell was to guard a satellite airfield where planes would do 'circuits and bumps'. We were not allowed outside the control tower – two of us on this duty for the weekend. A V-bomber came in, touched down and took off again. A little while later I looked out of the window and lo and behold, on the runway stood a donkey. I phoned the duty officer at Cranwell: "I'm reporting from the control tower at Welbeck, sir," and told him about the donkey. "Go and get it off then," he said, so I pointed out that we were not allowed to leave the tower, and that about 20 minutes before a V-bomber had been doing circuits and bumps. He asked if I had the number of the V-bomber but I hadn't – it was going too fast.

By this time another donkey had joined the first – duly reported. A little while later a rotund policeman on a bike peddled down the runway, trying to get rid of the donkeys. The owners of the donkeys then turned up and managed to take them away.

Thank goodness the V-bomber had not returned.

Most of the time at Cranwell I was going out with Elizabeth and I wanted to get engaged because I had inklings that I must be posted abroad at some stage. When you first go into the RAF you put down where you would like to go. So I put Australia (for the cricket – that would have been Darwin so would not have been a very good move anyway -), Germany and somewhere else. Anyway, I got posted to Singapore. Brilliant. I bought a ring and popped the question at the Norwood Rooms (which will come back in another experience). We got engaged. I don't know whether it went down too well with Fred – as I was an RAF bloke – but they were all good at the farm. My first time at the farm I ended up sitting down at a table with about twenty other people – what an ordeal. I broke a cup, helping to wash up. Oh dear!. They had a big Wolseley and I used to go to church in the afternoon in my mini, and as the Wolseley turned into the gate I swept inside and beat them. I was not popular with grandma. I was excommunicated, more or less. The farm was very good.

When I got posted to Singapore, Elizabeth was still at school. She was eighteen and I must have been twenty – two. There were one or two eyebrows raised but we just went out together and enjoyed life.

In a way, I was sad to go, but it was obviously going to be an experience. Elizabeth was pressing on with her A levels and I was getting ready to go. People said – rubber trees, snakes – never heard of them playing cricket or football - I wondered what on earth I was going to. We left from Luton airport on a propeller plane. It took ages. My first stop was Istanbul – I saw the mosque – sent a card to my mother. We then stopped at Bombay - now Mumbai– nearly missed the plane arguing with a bloke about cricket. It was monsoon time – unbelievable – flooding all over the place. From Mumbai I went to Columbo, which is now Sri Lanka. I couldn't believe how hot and sticky it was. As we went from Columbo to Singapore we went down the straits of Malacca – lightening all over the place. Unbelievable. Anyway, we got to Singapore – what a different world that is. Someone said; "You are posted to Tenga". There was another bloke with me – Bob Partner – who became a very good friend. We got there and got mosquito nets – which didn't seem to do much good (the mosquitoes seemed to like me) and we walked down to town. We could hear all the creatures croaking at each other – which was alien to us. I worked with a Javelin squadron at Tenga. They had about six or seven Javelins. If it rained, they didn't work. You pressed the button and the drop tank would fall off. The electrics would not work.

They obviously knew I was reasonable at football, but I was not allowed to play for a month, so that I could get acclimatised. In World War 2, Norfolk and Suffolk regiments went out to fight the Japanese two days after they had landed. What chance had they got? I played after a month - a half a game of football. My perspiration – because I had not put any Vaseline above my eyes – ran down like a bucket of water. Everybody watched the football under the lights. I walked into my section, and they said "You have been posted". I had only been there for five minutes. Bob and I had been posted. Bob was quite a good footballer, and we both played. We had been posted to Seletar – Maintenance Unit. Some bloke went past and said "You lucky so and so's". I had worked at Cranwell calibrating instruments, so obviously that was the place for me to go. Also, set hours, no nights – wonderful. So I went to this section. I walked into this office and the warrant officer said "I know you – I booked you at Waddington. Right – you are in my football team. You are captain. I want to see this GRS team get going". So I was captain and Bob was there with me – it was just inter-section games but very big rivalry. I managed to get into the second eleven for Seletar. The standard was very high. There were a lot of FEAF players – Far East Air Force – some ex-semi pros etc. I learned a lot. We played under lights and I played against an army eleven and a navy eleven. And the bloke in front of me in the navy eleven – I was centre half – played for Portsmouth Reserves, would you believe. Thank you very much and goodnight – no chance.

I was posted to Seletar, to 390MU, calibrating instruments mostly for plane cockpits. We lived in large apartment blocks recently built over mosquito swamps. We were eight to an air-conditioned room – this is significant. I soon went and visited the church on a Sunday and my Sundays became Holy Communion at 8a.m., back for breakfast then a dash across the island for 10 a.m. start for cricket (the football and cricket seasons were at the same time).

Mostly the cricket was played on the Pedang in front of the Government buildings at one end of which was the Singapore Rec Club, which anyone could join. At the other end was the Singapore C.C. based in a Victorian building. Jackets and ties had to be worn on entry, only members could buy drinks and in those days (1960s) a punkah wallah was still operating (fan). I sang in the church choir and carried the cross. One Good Friday I took the cross to put in its place near the altar, having removed the muslin which had covered it. I took the cross up on Easter Sunday – nothing was said.

Easter Monday – day off. Tuesday morning, I walked into work and was told to report to the padre. I went to his office to be confronted by the padre and the Group Captain. The Padre asked me what I had done with the muslin that had covered the cross so I said I had taken it off and put it on one side – I thought someone had put it over the cross to keep it clean after they had polished it, whereupon the Group Captain looked as if he was about to take off without his aircraft! The Padre asked if my church at home was a High or a Low church. I thought better of making a crack about having a high tower and said sort of medium, so the smile came back to the Group Captain's face. They explained to me that in some churches (High), during Holy Week all statues and crosses etc are covered – obviously this hadn't happened in Loddon.

Not long after, the vacancy for the George Club manager came up. This club was attached to the church and was a place for people to have sausage and chips, drinks – but no alcohol – and a library. The manager lived on the premises, in his own quarters, including a shower, and oversaw staff and the general running of the club – in addition to his normal job on the station. I was appointed to the job, which was wonderful.

Various things went on at the church, large fetes raising money for local charities, a Burns Night and a drama group. I was also chairman of the Anglican Young People's Association and organised various speakers, one of whom was the Governor of the notorious Changhi Jail.

Once the doors clanged behind me wow, what a place! I visited the chapel, which all the tourists go to. From there we went around the prison workshops where all the prisoners had to stop work and line up facing the wall. It was at the time when the Great Train Robbers seemed to have no difficulty escaping from British prisons so I asked if anyone had ever escaped from Changhi. The Governor said:

"No, only the inner wall. We shot him in the leg." He then pointed out the machine guns at each corner of the outer walls. It was an experience but I was pleased to get out again.

The job I was doing, calibrating instruments, was interesting. We had to do lots of modifications to improve efficiency.

In my job as George Club manager I had to supervise deliveries of food and drink and might, therefore, be late arriving for work. There was a clampdown on people being late so I made sure I was always on my bike as soon as deliveries had been received.

I played football and cricket for the station but a lot of people had no hobbies and just sat around drinking in their off-duty time. Bob and I decided we would visit the Cameron Highland in Malaysia – about 6,000ft above sea level. We stayed in a hotel which wasn't very nice and we used out travel warrants on the train. We didn't stay too long but I noticed a Rest House, which looked more pleasant and I resolved to stay there on my next visit.

We were offered three travel warrants a year and not many people chose to use theirs. I made full use of mine and travelled by first-class sleeper to Ipo and stayed at the Rest House – roaring fires, carnations and a cool climate – just like England, Jumpers on!

The only downside of the Rest House was its situation, across the road from a mosque, which called people to prayer at 5 a.m. When I looked out just before 5 no-one appeared to be walking towards the mosque, so I thought I would investigate. Next morning I got up at 4.45 a.m., stood outside the mosque while the call to prayer was issued and at the end of it was a loud 'click' – clearly a recorded message on a timer – no-one in sight!

One morning, a chap was sitting on a wall outside the Rest House and said he was giving a talk in the afternoon and would I like to go. With nothing else planned I went along and sat at the back. After the meeting an elderly lady asked where I came from and I said "Singapore". She replied: "No, no, I mean in the UK." I told her Loddon and she asked if I knew Paul Clements. "Yes" I said, "I used to play cricket with him," and she told me she was his aunt. She asked where I was staying, told me to pack up and go and stay at her mission house further into the hills.

Her mission house was a respite home where missionaries who were working in other countries in the area (such as China) could go to relax.

Another time that I was in the Cameron Highlands, a Major was staying at the Rest House at the same time and he was obviously a member of the local golf club and invited me to play with him. I told him I wasn't very good at golf. He must have thought I was being modest and said: "Come along anyway". He took the first shot and whacked it straight down the middle – my shot disappeared under the deckchairs where the lady members were sitting. A brilliant off-drive if I'd been playing cricket.

"Oh dear," said the Major. "I'll go off with this caddy, you take the other and I'll meet up with you later." My next shot wasn't too bad and we managed to progress to the third tee, taking about six or seven shots, when the caddy said: "In view of your last shot, we should let the next party through." I said I didn't think it was a bad shot but he insisted we should let the next party through. I asked who it was, to which he replied: "The Prime Minister (of Malaya)" with his pros, who raised their hats to us in acknowledgement and carried on.

It took me an hour or so to get round the course. I met the Major in the bar and he bought me an orange squash. Just as we were leaving I met the Prime Minister, who asked what did I think of the Big Pull Out (British troops being withdrawn from Malaysia) and I replied that I was enjoying my time in Malaysia but it was up to people like him to make that sort of decision.

Back at the Rest House we had fish sandwiches etc in a temperature of about 60F deg while in Singapore it was 80F deg. I was having a lovely time in the Highlands but had to return to Singapore, travelling by train through vast rubber plantations.

When I got back to camp there was a letter waiting for me from Elizabeth, saying if I didn't want to write to her occasionally then we could both go our separate ways. This upset me very much, probably because I'd been having such a pleasant time in the Cameron Highlands.

That night I had a football match under lights and next day I met Sqn. Ldr De Thier who said: " You didn't play very well last night, what's the matter with you?" So I told him and he said: "Stupid boy". I had to agree.

On the Monday morning when I walked into the section the sergeant said I was to report to the Wing Co. so I was to go and get my best blues on and go back for inspection. I went off to see the Wing Co. Who said: "I hear you've been a stupid boy". I said: "If you're referring to not writing to my fiancée then yes, that's right". He sent me to Sqn. Ldr. De Thier who said: "We need an aircraft weighing machine taking to the UK. This is usually done by an officer but in view of you running the George Club so well we thought you could take this machine to Swanton Morley. Is that anywhere near you?" "Yes", I said. "Only about 20 miles away." "Right" he said. "You take this machine to Swanton Morley," and he gave me the details.

I was to leave next day on a VC10 from Changhi. I found my seat at the front of the plane – in fact one for me and one for the instrument - and off we went. Our first stop was Bahrain, where on leaving the plane I had to take the machine with me. There was coffee in the waiting room but my chief memory of Bahrain was the heat of the tarmac coming through my shoes. Transport Command did not do meals on board the plane but the meal was left under your seat. We were told by the crew to look under our seats for our meals when we boarded. Obviously they had not realised that the machine occupied one seat so there was one meal for me and another for the machine! I ate both, whereupon I received a tap on my shoulder and turned round to see the AOC and his wife. He remarked that I played for the station at cricket and football and asked if the package had enjoyed its meal. I laughed.

The next stop was Tehran.

On arriving at Lyneham, a card was held up with my name on it. A staff car was waiting to take me and the machine to Norfolk. I asked if anyone else was travelling to Norfolk and two hands went up. I said they could travel with me in the staff car whereupon one of them said to me:"Who on earth are you?" I said: "Never mind who I am, just get in the car", having checked with the driver who said it was no problem at all. Off we went.

Things to note, Radio Caroline and the greenness of the fields.
We went straight to Swanton Morley where I left the machine to be locked up in the guardroom and I had to return a day or two later to be given details of my return flight to Singapore.

Somehow I got a message through to meet up at Thorpe Station where my mother and Elizabeth were waiting for me and we went home to Loddon. We were all pleased to see each other.

On reporting back to Swanton Morley I was told to report to Movements, knocked on the sliding door whereupon it was a chap I used to know at Wymondham College. He asked me what I was doing there so I said I had left a machine to be recalibrated and must return on the first flight with 2 seats available. "Well," he said "I've only got one seat on the plane leaving in two days but there will be two free seats next week." I said: "OK" and went home again – having nine days at home, taking lots of photographs of Norfolk to show the missionaries in the Highlands on my return to Malaysia – when I would make sure to write home this time!

I was put on a flight from Luton airport, another staff car first but there was only one seat so I had to carry the machine on my lap. Only one meal each stop! On arrival at Payaleva Airport I was met by a staff car and taken to Seletar – the machine again locked up in the guardroom. The next day I returned it to Sqn. Ldr. De Thier, who said: "I thought you might have been back sooner," so I explained the situation.

Far East Air Force Cricket Cup

Seletar 1st team won. I held a good catch against Ghan. Towards the end of the cricket season it was decided to hold a Seletar C.C. dinner dance, but you had to have a female with you. I didn't want to risk upsetting my fiancée again but I was expected to be there. In the end I asked a WRAF who spoke a bit like me but with a West Country accent. I explained the situation and she said: "Anything for a free dinner dance!" so off we went for an enjoyable evening. I thought no more about it.

A couple of years later I was playing cricket at Yarmouth and on the other side, Old Yarmouthians, was a chap called Wayne Allen. At the end of his bowling mark, before he bowled to me, he shouted: "Your girlfriend is on at the Theatre Royal." I asked him what he meant and he said: "That bird you took to the dinner dance in Singapore is Pam Ayres and she is on at the Theatre Royal." By then she had left the RAF and launched a new career in entertainment- so I had taken Pam Ayres out to dinner.

Trip to Thailand

My friend Bob and I decided to take a week's leave to visit the island of Penang, which had RAF accommodation, about four to a room, right next to the sea. We booked a day train journey to Kuala Lumpur and it turned out the train was made in Coventry. We stopped at a junction called Gemas. To the left would be Kuala Lumpur – to the east, the sea. I asked the conductor how long the train would stay in the station and he said half an hour. I told Bob I was going to look at the engine and I chatted to the driver, who asked if I would like to come aboard. Would I?! He showed me all the controls and then asked if I would like a cup of tea, whereupon a boy in shorts was despatched and came back with a Heinz beans tin with lid folded back, containing my tea.

I went back to the carriage with Bob to continue our journey to Kuala Lumpur where we spent the first night of our holiday. We caught an early morning train to Butterworth where we were on the border between Malaya and Thailand. We took the ferry to Penang, which was very crowded with lots of animals, goats, cars, buses etc. We spotted a concrete bottomed boat which had run aground on a wooden pylon.

Arriving in Georgetown, the capital of Penang, an RAF bus took us to the other side of the island, which was just as you imagine – a tropical paradise. We thought we would hire a couple of bikes and somehow reached the highest point on the island amongst pineapple plantations. We looked down at the sea and set ourselves the challenge (having first tested the brakes) of freewheeling down to the sea – about two miles – going carefully round the bends and sometimes meeting cars coming up the other way. We arrived safely at Georgetown in time for lunch.

The next day we hired a rowing boat. There was a small island off Penang we thought we would explore. There were warnings that the tides were tricky but had no problem rowing to the island, where we met some monks. However, on our return journey we met the rip tides which made rowing really hard work. Eventually we reached the shore and agreed never to do that again. We were totally exhausted. The rest of the day we rested on the beach.

The following day we visited the various temples on the island, the first being the Temple of the Sacred Turtles, some looked as if they had been there for a hundred years – as did the water they were swimming in. We proceeded to climb to the top of the temple, each stage costing us another dollar. It was a lovely view from the top – and we didn't have to pay on the way down.
Next was the Temple of the Sacred Snakes, where they were fed eggs, which you could see progressing through them.

The main temple contained the statue of the Golden Buddha, which was entirely covered in gold leaf. It was lying on its side and was about 20 ft high. Behind this reclining Buddha were compartments on shelves which people could purchase to contain their ashes at a later date. Outside was a sign which we thought was a Nazi symbol but we were assured that it was back-to-front and a sign of peace. The inside of the temple was immaculately kept.

The next day we travelled on the Penang hill railway which was a very steep climb with good views from the top. It was a rack and pinion railway (like Snowdon's) and we came down slowly. Having had an enjoyable week we returned to Seletar.

Not long after we were back at work I was summoned to the phone. Sqn. Ldr. Andrews, who was in charge of the Beverley flight – and in charge of cricket – said to find two other reliable people for supernumerary crew. Where were we going? Bangkok! We were needed for loading and unloading equipment and were expected to be away for three days with accommodation in an hotel. It didn't take long to find two friends to go with me.

A View of the Penang Hill Railway

A View of the Penang Hill Railway

We loaded the equipment, flew to Bangkok, unloaded and went to the hotel. That night there was a World Championship boxing match – I think Walter McGowan was fighting a boxer from Thailand. Before this bout there was a kick-boxing match – red shorts v. blue shorts. Lots of people had bet on the blue shorts winning but, unfortunately, red shorts won. Cue a mass brawl and punch-up. The police surrounded our small party and said: "Sit down, it will all end soon." The King walked in and the fighting stopped immediately; people sat down because everyone had to be lower than the King. The Thai boxer won, to our relief and we returned safely to our hotel.

The next day, while we were sitting by the pool, an officer arrived to tell us there were engine problems with our plane so we would have to stay an extra five days – oh dear!

We hired a guide who took us to the Imperial Palace and the Temple of Dawn, where we thought we would climb to the top. Sadly the last section was via a rusty-looking ladder so we changed our minds.

We visited other temples, all Buddhist, which were truly magnificent in appearance. At one, we approached an open door and inside it was very dark, with a humming noise, made by the monks with their prayer wheels. One of the monks outside, speaking perfect English, asked if I would like to take his photograph. He had been educated at Oxford and was then doing his National Service with no salary – being a monk –but living on charitable donations.

The next place we visited was the floating market of Bangkok where you could buy vegetables from passing boats. There were shops, made of wood, on the river bank where you could buy such things as Thai silk. I spotted what I thought was a lovely piece of silk which changed colour (green to blue) as it moved. I bought this for Elizabeth and thought she might have it made up into something for a going-away outfit after our wedding. We were asked if we were Americans or English because the English price was lower than the one charged to Americans. There were quite a lot of Americans around, on leave from the Vietnam War. They had a few stories to tell!

We then got back in the boat and proceeded to the Royal Boat House where the royal barge was kept. The whole boat was covered in gold leaf and was used by the king and his entourage when he was visiting around his area. There were lots of waterways through Bangkok and many shanty towns. When our Queen visited Thailand she was not allowed to go in this boat as it was considered unsafe.

After an enjoyable time in Bangkok we re-loaded the plane – by now repaired – and returned to Seletar.

Although I was coming towards the end of my posting to Singapore, it was a very busy period of football and cricket finals. I had been asked to submit a list of all the activities undertaken while at Seletar, apart from work. Manager of the George Club, chairman of the Young People's Association, 1st and 2nd XI cricket, playing in the Far East Air Force Association finals and winning; playing for 1st and 2nd XI football teams, church activities and Seletar Choral Society which performed all over the island, including at the National Theatre.

During one of the football finals I was injured towards the end of the game and taken to the medical centre. While I was being treated the medic said: "You must be someone important, the Station Commander has just been in to see how you are!"

Not long afterwards I was presented with the Station Commander's award for recreational and social activities. As well as the shield, one of the advantages was being able to choose which station to go to on returning to the UK. Since I only had a year and a half left of my nine years I chose Coltishall – which was nearest to my home. Elizabeth was completing her teacher training at Keswick College, Norwich and we planned to marry in the summer when she completed her course.

Elizabeth and I were married in July 1968 at Sisland Church with a reception at the farm. For her going-away outfit Elizabeth wore the Thai silk made into a dress and jacket by the dressmaker who had made the wedding dress. We travelled to Skye for our honeymoon before settling into our bungalow at Horstead.

At Coltishall, as well as working on the Lightnings I, of course, played cricket and football and had lived on camp until we were married. During this time I had to consider what I would do on leaving the RAF in September 1969. I decided to apply to Keswick College to do a teacher training course with PE as my main subject. This came as something of a surprise to my officers since I was not regarded as an academic but I thought I would give it a go. I was invited for interviews and offered a place, to the surprise of some!

Life at Coltishall was comparatively mundane compared with Seletar but I was playing football and cricket for local clubs at weekends - Norwich Wanderers for cricket and YMCA for football on Saturday in winter.

I had left the RAF, handed in my uniform and 1250, I was cutting the lawn one day when Elizabeth came to the door and said there was a phone call from RAF Coltishall. Would I play cricket? I thought they meant that afternoon but no. I had to go to Coltishall next morning and fly to Leucars, near Dundee, for an RAF Cup match. When we got off the plane at Leucars I was met by three or four chaps I worked with in Singapore – a pleasant reunion. We stayed overnight on the camp but visited Dundee in the evening. Part of the town still had gas lamps in 1969. Next day we played cricket and were heavily defeated – I scored no runs and took no wickets – I hope I fielded well. We returned to Coltishall and so ended my career in the RAF.

Teacher Training

I was ready to start my teacher training at Keswick College where my main subject was PE. As it was a junior/secondary course I also had to do several subsidiary subjects such as Geography, Art, Science and everyone had to do English, Maths and RE, as well as Education.

Physical Education involved a wide range of sports, not only cricket and football but also swimming, gymnastics, canoeing, rock climbing, country dancing, basketball, hockey etc. Sailing on Filby Broad and camping in the Southwold area were novel and memorable experiences.
(Appendix – notes made at the time)

We had to do two Special Studies, one for our main subject and the other concerning Education in general.

During the last year or so of my teacher training I also became churchwarden for the first time, at Horstead. The other churchwarden, the Rector and I were all about the same age – in our late twenties. The older members of the congregation didn't seem to mind especially since some of our involvement was with the recently-opened Horstead Conference House which was very busy at times.

A discussion about the Conference House, between the churchwardens and the

Archdeacon of Norwich was necessary at one point. I can't remember what was discussed but I do remember the dinner at Heggatt Hall with the Archdeacon sitting in the middle of a very long table with Richard Gurney at one end and me at the other, The meal included pheasant and I seemed to get rather a lot of the pellets which shot it and they made a lot of noise as I dropped them onto my plate.

Towards the end of my first year at college I was playing cricket at weekends at Cromer. Trevor Reynolds, another player, worked at Norfolk Canneries and asked if I would be interested in a job for a few weeks at the beginning of my summer holiday from college. The job entailed travelling around local farms which grew strawberries, estimating how many strawberries would be sent to the factory that day. For some it would be tons and for others, just a few pallets. The usual reps were busy with the pea harvest – critical as it was essential to harvest and process the peas at exactly the right moment of ripeness.

A car, of sorts, was provided and I roared around North Norfolk finding the farms and estimating the strawberry crops. I did this for the three years that I was at college during the first few weeks of the summer holiday.

During my time at Keswick, Henry Crabtree, from Essex, did a Level 1 cricket course for those of us interested. I passed this course, managed to complete my college course and gain my certificate and took up a post at Hoveton School.

From Hoveton I took three or four boys who were interested to Wensum Lodge for cricket coaching one evening a week. The course was run by John Shepherd, who asked me to help with the coaching and so began my involvement with Norfolk Schools Cricket. Gordon Blyth, chairman of the Norfolk Schools' Cricket Association, asked me to help him run the Norfolk Under-15s and over time I became their manager. Gordon and I travelled the country, both with the Under 15 teams and to the AGMs of the England Schools' Cricket Association, which were always held in smart hotels in such places as Durham, Nottingham, Hove and even, when Gordon became chairman of the England Schools, organising our own event in Norwich.

Towards the end of my year at Hoveton I walked into school and Mr Church, the headmaster, told me to go and look at Reepham High School, where they were expecting me. I was ushered straight into the head's office and asked if I would like to run the PE Department at the school. Of course I would, so they told me to put on a jacket and tie (at this initial meeting I was still wearing a tracksuit) and go back the next day for an official interview. During the tour of the school I met the deputy head Jim Howard, who recognised me from a British Legion event where we had both been involved in entertaining, Jim with his funny stories and Elizabeth and I singing.

Next day, after parking the car, two older gentlemen got out of their cars and one said to the other: "I don't know why we've been asked to come as there's only one bloke turning up." I thought I might stand a chance!

I was shown to the headmaster's study where a ring of people sat. The chairman of the governors was a lady, very smartly dressed including a splendiferous hat, but before she had time to open her mouth, one of the gentlemen said: "I know this man, he played cricket for Norwich Wanderers – he's the man we need." Madam Chairman was insisting that the interview hadn't started yet but within a quarter of an hour I had been offered the job and accepted.

That was a memorable summer because in July '73 our daughter Catherine was born. She had 'clicky' hips and had to wear a brace for two months which meant weekly visits to the Norfolk and Norwich Hospital. When I had asked Elizabeth to marry me she told me that she 'knew' she was going to have a handicapped child (no family history or medical reason) and we thought perhaps Catherine was going to be lame but, fortunately, the brace did its work and all was well.
Over the first winter at Reepham, I worked hard to sort out the football teams and raised money to buy a set of football shirts. One boy could play cricket and between us we found enough players to form a team to play against other schools. Against Fakenham High, Reepham were all out for 87, Peter Wilkinson 86 not out. The other run was a bye. We won by 10 runs somehow.

Thinking we might try basketball I asked Mr Sibson at Wells if we could watch one of his school's matches on a Saturday morning. The coach turned up to take several of us, including a boy named Pike with an enormous haversack on his back. "What have you got there?" I asked and he replied: "Sandwiches sir, cos my dad says it's a long way to Wales!" In those days many of the children had not travelled far from their home villages. Going to Wells was quite an adventure, never mind the basketball.

So we progressed slowly and built up various sports teams, helped by a wonderful groundsman, John Barber, who was delighted that we were going to play cricket. Mr Wise, the Headmaster, was very supportive and we managed to win a few games.

In my first year at Reepham I was told it was our turn to organise the Area Sports (athletics). I said I would do it and Don Rayner, from Aylsham, was very helpful because he was pleased I had agreed Reepham would do it. Reepham's games mistress, Gerry, was also very helpful and between us we managed to organise the event.

By 1975 one of the Reepham boys was particularly good at running. Mark Abigail had a deformed arm as the result of Thalidomide and could not manage to play cricket successfully so concentrated on running. By the time of the County Sports, if he managed the qualifying time on the day he would be going to the All-England Championships.

The County Sports were to be held at Downham Market where I was in charge of the pole vault. Other members of staff and about 20 other pupils set off. I had already had a busy morning dropping off Elizabeth at North Walsham Hospital where she insisted she was properly well cared-for to give birth to our baby while I supported Mark in his efforts. Catherine was being looked after by Elizabeth's mother.

I rang the hospital several times during the day to be told, around lunchtime, that we had a boy but there was a problem – he had Down's syndrome – should he tell Elizabeth? I said: "Yes, she is half expecting it." One of the staff with me was an atheist and said he wouldn't know what to do in that situation but I had a faith to rely on, which was really helpful. Reepham's PE mistress, Sue, had rung Reepham School with the news and the Deputy Head, John Ames, drove to Downham to pick me up and take me back to school. When we arrived, the place was in silence – the Head had locked himself in his room and no-one knew what to say to me.

I drove to North Walsham Hospital to be met by a nurse we knew through our association with the local Liberal Party – who flung her arms around me and said: "Why you?" Then she took me to a lovely sunny side ward where I was greeted by a smiling Elizabeth saying: "Come and look at our little boy," and I was so relieved to see them both.

Mark ran his qualifying time and later went to the All-England Championships.

A few days later we were drawn in a cricket Cup Match against Wymondham College, my old school. We played away and Peter Wilkinson and Tim Saunders scored a lot of runs, the boys fielded superbly to defeat Wymondham – an unexpected result. John Shepherd, who managed Wymondham, said: "They've done it for you".

About a year earlier I had been on an Advanced Coaches course at Scarborough, at John's suggestion. Most of the people on the course were Minor Counties or First Class Counties players. In one session I had to teach 20 girls how to play the pull shot and organise it so that they didn't hit each other. After many sessions I did not pass the course but it had been a very valuable experience and hard work.

My disappointment was lifted on returning home to find that in my absence Catherine had started to walk a few steps. This was a big relief after having had clicky hips.

Elizabeth and I had always sung in school and church choirs but during my time at RAF Coltishall we teamed up with a guitarist called Sid to do some entertaining at village hall events and old people's homes etc. This came to an end soon after I left Coltishall but Elizabeth and I continued to do some unaccompanied singing at various events.

Our Rector at Horstead asked us to do a few songs at the Sparrow's Nest Theatre in Lowestoft for a Songs of Praise evening, including a song with him which we had not actually practiced together. Peeping out at the audience before we began we realised that the theatre was full and were told that there were almost 1,000 people there. Time for some nerves – but all went well.

Another big occasion was when we were asked to do a half-hour slot while the band had a rest during a dinner-dance at the Norwood Rooms in Norwich. We were asked by Mr and Mrs Nash, who we knew through the Royal British Legion and had assumed it was a Legion do but oh no! We had been told to dress ourselves up, DJ etc and found that it was a Masonic event. The only person there that we knew, apart from the Nashes, who were presiding, was our bank manager. He was on table 35 and seemed a little surprised to learn that we were on the top table. Bet he was even more surprised later when we did our turn!

It cannot have been too bad because we were later asked to a Masonic event at Wroxham. By that time we had Catherine, who we took along in her carrycot and we left her sleeping in the Masonic Chamber while we did our stint.

Between times, a fellow performer had introduced us to his agent, Peachy Mead, who sent us to do the interval at a Bingo session at Gorleston Casino. Being paid was something of a novelty but we couldn't charge for most of the things that we continued to do.

After Catherine and Neil were born we didn't do much by way of singing except very locally on odd occasions.

During the spring of 1975 I had been troubled by sciatica and found playing cricket painful. I was asked to play cricket for Coltishall who said they would understand if I had suddenly to call off (if Neil was ill) and somehow I found I was captain. One of the other players was Mel Machin, who also played football for Norwich City (later manager of Manchester City among other clubs) and he and his family were very supportive and encouraging during our early years with Neil.

In fact we were blessed with a great deal of help from family, neighbours and church friends. Hardly a day went by without someone calling in.

I was invited to have another try at the Advanced Coaches Course (cricket) this time to be held at Lilleshall in Staffordshire, not far from Jo Machin's family home so she decided if I was going there she and their daughter Luisa would have a lift.

Halfway through the course I felt like giving up because it seemed so difficult I thought I would fail again. During a phone call to Elizabeth she pointed out that Jo and Luisa would be disappointed so I decided to see it out. Roger Tolchard suggested that if I showed a group of fellow candidates (mainly First Class cricketers) how to organise a group of 20 children in various tasks then they would help me with my demonstrations. We stayed up late helping each other out. Teamwork paid off and I received my certificate as an Advanced Coach.

I was now Manager of Norfolk Schools Under-15 side playing matches against Suffolk, Lincolnshire, Yorkshire, Nottinghamshire and in some years there were tours based in places such as Chepstow and Leek, Staffs. These took up the summer half-term holiday and the first few weeks of the school summer holiday. Coaching took place each year during the Easter holiday at Wymondham College with days for Trials following on.

On one occasion when were playing Leicestershire at Empingham, the Leics Under-15 manager suggested that, if I agreed, he would propose me as the next Midlands Under-15 manager. At the next Midlands Area Meeting I was duly proposed and elected. My area was from Norfolk to the Welsh border and from Notts' northern border to north of Oxford. Needless to say we had two trials, one in the west at Shrewsbury School and the eastern one at Beacon Road, Loughborough and the final trial was also at Loughborough.

One day at the final trial, the only selector to turn up for the Midlands team trial was me. This meant, on my own, I was in charge of 20 boys plus parents.

One of the fathers said: "I can see you've got problems. I'll umpire all day except when my son is batting," and promptly went out and set up the stumps and bails. Brian Reynolds, coach of Northamptonshire, trundled through the gate in his car and I went over and spoke to him. I told him of the difficulties and said I would speak to him at lunchtime about the various boys' abilities and he said: "Why don't you ask the man who is umpiring what he thinks? He is M.J.K. Smith, who has captained Warwickshire and England." And so the trial proceeded and I picked 14 players to represent the Midlands.

My first match as Midlands manager was against Wales, which was one of their trials at Bishop Vesey School. One of the teachers from Bishop Vesey's was Rex Warbank, who among his other jobs was the announcer at Edgebaston and he said if ever I was at Edgebaston I could come and sit with him in his box, which of course I did at the first suitable occasion.

Many years later, after I had retired from full-time teaching and was doing supply, I was asked to accompany a school party from Reepham High School who were going to a Test Match at Edgebaston between England and the West Indies. I met Hugh Cherry, who was on the Warwickshire Committee and he remembered me from my days with Midland Schools.. He invited me into the Committee area of the Pavilion and I sat in the area above the clock with the Chairman of Hampshire Cricket Club and on the other side, the Chairman of the West Indies Cricket Board and we had an interesting conversation about youngsters playing cricket and coaching them. Jasper Carrott sat just behind us – it was a memorable day!

The Midlands meetings used to take place at Edgebaston and Trent Bridge which very often coincided with a County one-day game in the afternoon, which we stayed to watch.

After a few years as Midlands Under-15 Team Manager, I was asked to be the Midlands representative as England selector – choosing theUnder-15 team and taking them to matches against Wales and Scotland.

I was at Beckenham, in Kent, where both Under-19 and Under-15 teams had been playing matches against Scotland. Someone from the committee asked me to drive a mini-bus with some Under-19s and Under-15s to their next matches in Wales. I had a short practice driving the bus, without any boys, before loading up and heading off, in the rain, to Wales. Travelling along the M4 was a rather anxious time with six or seven boys who would go on to become Test cricketers as well as several First Class county players.

Another memorable occasion was the England School's Festival in Cornwall. The first game was Midlands versus the West at Helpston. On arrival at the ground we were greeted by the police, informing us that the groundsman had died in the pavilion. We were told to take the boys away somewhere, so we decided to see if we could visit Goonhilly, an early-warning station on the Lizard. We were taken for a look round and after about an hour or so returned to the cricket ground where we were surprised to find that the body had been taken away and the widow was getting lunch ready as she insisted that was what her husband would have wanted!

Chris Twort, John Wake and I went out to have a look at the square, which was too damp to start the game. I realised that just across the road was the naval helicopter station and I remembered that in Singapore we had used a helicopter to dry the square by hovering over it. The Chairman of England Schools overheard me talking about this and immediately got on the phone and said: "You Air Force fellows…." until I pointed out they were the Navy, so he started again and asked them if they would help out by doing the same thing. They replied that they would come in about half an hour. They duly arrived and parked the helicopter in the out-field. I went over to the chap, who jumped out of the helicopter with a walkie-talkie. I explained to him what had happened in Singapore and just before the pilot took off I realised that the stumps were still on the pitch and raced to recover them before they were flung round the field. The helicopter hovered over the square and did the job, enough for us to play.

The game duly began and proceeded until tea-time, whereupon the other game, between the South and North, which was to have taken place at another ground,

had been called off and the boys and staff had come to see what was happening with our game. They were surprised that we had managed to start. The Chairman was telling the other officials how he had managed to organise it with the helicopter whereupon Cyril Cooper, Secretary of England Schools' Cricket, said: "Who's paying?!"

The next day at Truro I was watching a game between the President's XI and England Schools' XI. I had travelled to Truro by bus as Elizabeth needed the car. The MCC President came up to me and said: "Mike, we've booked you a 1st class ticket to go to Glasgow by train. You will transfer to a sleeper at Birmingham. What you have to do in Glasgow is to organise tickets from Glasgow to Northampton where they are playing against Wales." Having collected the tickets I was to go to Glasgow University and check out the accommodation. The next day I was to go to Pollock, where the game was to be played and check out the facilities, wicket etc.

I had told my mother I was due to go to Glasgow and she told me to try to find time to visit the Burrell Collection, also in Pollock.

After a wonderful journey, some of it beside the sea, at Dawlish, I arrived in Birmingham and found my sleeping compartment and I enjoyed the rest of the journey. At Glasgow Central I collected the tickets for Northampton, caught a taxi and went to Glasgow University. At reception I was told where our accommodation was and stayed there myself that night.

Next morning, a Sunday, I looked at a map to find the best route to Pollock and decided to walk there. I though there should be a short cut and had started on it when I was approached by a policeman who asked me where I was going. I told him I was going to Pollock to inspect the facilities for a cricket match. He said: I don't advise you to go that way sir. I'll show you where you can catch a bus." I caught the bus to Pollock and when I arrived I found a gentleman looking after the square and he turned out to be Omar Henry, who was the club pro, coach, groundsman etc but who had been a prominent figure in South African cricket during its transition.

We talked about the wicket and facilities and then he told me the Burrell Collection opening times so I strolled over to find the lovely surroundings, obtained a book for my mother and looked around myself. I came across a model of a cat, about the size of my thumb and asked a security man what would happen if I put it in my pocket. He said if I picked it up, shutters would come down, alarm bells ring and I would be on my way! Apparently it was priceless but there were lots of other wonderful things to see.

Catching a bus back to the University I sat beside a lady and we started to talk. She belonged to the Glasgow Orpheus Choir (now called the Phoenix Choir). It was so interesting that I missed my stop and had to walk back but I was there in time to meet the players and committee as they arrived.
The next unusual occurrence was on our journey from Glasgow to Northampton. Because of a railway workers' strike we had to change trains at Carstairs, so we had to unload all our equipment and stand on the platform to wait for another train. The Under-19s, including Atherton and Hussein decided to play forward defensive shots in the middle of a busy platform. Inevitably the ball went on the tracks but there seemed to be an endless supply of tennis balls.

We eventually reported to Northampton where we were met by John Wake, who took charge of proceedings there. We (the Under-15s) played at Northampton Saints' ground, which had allotments at one end. Ramprakash kept hitting the ball into the allotments when a man appeared and shouted: "Either take the off-spinner off or retire the batsman. I'm trying to do some gardening here." Needless to say this fell on deaf ears.

Catching a bus back to Norwich, I completed my round Britain tour.

The next memorable occasion was at Rugby School where the England Schools' Festival was being held that year. This year I travelled by train with Carl Rogers (a Reepham School pupil). Elizabeth needed the car to take Catherine and a friend from Taverham Hall School to Brandeston Prep School where they were staying for a week rehearsing for the National Prep Schools Orchestra concert at Snape Maltings.

Hubert Doggert, President of the England Schools' Cricket Association said he had been reading his paper that morning and had spotted the name Catherine Rowson in the Prep Schools' Orchestra – was that anything to do with me? I told him she was my daughter and he said: "Well, we've virtually picked the team, you need not be here, so off you go." I told him there was a small problem of not having a car there. He walked off, to return 10 minutes later and said that the team manager said I could borrow his car – an automatic, which I had never driven before. So I made my way to Snape – very carefully!

My own playing career

The first game I played, Mr Farrell was playing for Loddon and he got me to play – on a malting wicket. I took three wickets! I then went on to play regularly for Loddon on a Saturday and played quite well as a bowler. David Pearce, the postman, gave me a lot of encouragement. On a Sunday Egger Grint used to get our lads together to play for a team called Greaves XI at Yarmouth. He would pick us up in his van, which he compared to Jones' van on 'Dads' Army' but not as big. The back was tied up with string once we were all inside. One of the lads was Dougie Mattocks who played for Norfolk Minor Counties and also Notts County at football. This was a rickety old van – anything could happen!

One day, there was a screech and some sparks and we saw the back wheel proceeding down the road ahead of us. Egger went and got it, brought it back, undid the string to let us out and got his jacks, nuts and bolts etc to sort things out. He could turn his hand to anything! We jacked the van up, he screwed the back wheel on and we arrived only 15 minutes late. This didn't really matter as games could only start when the player who was in charge of Reedham Swing Bridge arrived anyway!

Mr Greaves was a very eccentric man who would turn up on his bike and play in his whites still wearing his cycle clips. One day a chap turned up with his dog and on that day we had only nine men in the team. Greaves told the man with the dog – who had only come to watch – to tie the dog up, he was next in! The man tied up his dog and received instructions to "swish it around a bit". He got about 20 runs, untied his dog and walked off!

I played cricket for Wymondham College – mostly for the 2nd XI at an average level but when I returned from Singapore, having developed my sporting skills in the RAF, I decided I would try to improve my lot by playing a higher standard of cricket. One day, I was in Pilch's shop in Norwich, when Mr George Pilch suggested I should try out for Norwich Wanderers.

So I went to the Wanderers, at Barton Turf, near Wroxham and my first game was for their 3rd XI. I took five wickets and the next week was in the 1st XI on a Sunday, against a very good team from Suffolk – William Brown's. They had several county players – I was hit all over the place and soon found out what senior cricket was all about!

At Wanderers, I seemed regularly to be picked for away matches and I became rather tired of this so when Eric Bedwell, at Cromer, asked me to play for them, I said yes. They were a senior Norfolk side with some county players.

It was very pleasant playing for Cromer; I alternated between the 1st and 2nd teams and played in some Carter Cup matches. Elizabeth used to score for Cromer and one day she was actually serving lunch and scoring at the same time! Tony Lawes, a lovely chap, suggested that she could also run the roller up and down while she was about it! I once took 9 wickets against Gothic, bowling up the hill and against the wind, for the 2nd XI. We sometimes had big crowds – when the tide came in and brought a mist over the beach.

Dick Wright then asked me to play for Overstrand on Sundays. By this time Elizabeth was heavily pregnant. We played a touring side and at the end of the game they always gave out "fines" and Man of the Match. I got Man of the Match and was presented with a tie. The chap scoring for the touring team was fined – for scoring in a score box with a lady scorer and, in addition, fined for not scoring in a score box with a lady scorer!

Coltishall Cricket Club asked me to play for them but I was reluctant as Neil had recently been born. Eventually I was persuaded and when I turned up, a chap called Smithson (who was groundsman at Trowse for Norwich City) was captain of the side. However, he told me on my arrival that I was to be captain. I tried to decline but he was very modest and said I could place a field better than him – so I became captain of Coltishall. On a number of occasions we had Norwich City footballers playing for us, including Mel Machin and Martin Peters. Once, we went to pick up Martin Peters at his house. Mel went to the door, came back alone and said: "Come on, the ten men!" Martin's wife had said he could not play as he had to go shopping!

One of the boys I had in my school team was called Peter Wilkinson, and he asked me to play for Horsford. At one stage I was captain for a while as the previous captain, Alan Hardy, had broken his leg. I captained several Carter Cup quarter and semi-finals; I also captained the team in the inaugural Bliss Cup final against Barleycorns, who had a number of good players in their side. We played at Vauxhall Mallards and, against all the odds, we managed to win!

I became chairman of Horsford when I gave up playing. I also became Team Manager of the Under-13's who went to the finals of the Under-13 Cup at Oakham School and won the whole competition. Two years later I was Team Manager of the Under-15s team which won the Harry Seacombe Cup for the whole of the county, at Basingstoke. 1500 teams had entered! While I was chairman of Horsford we won the Carter Cup, with Steve Read as captain.

Richard Taylor, a teacher at Taverham High School, was in charge of coaching on a Sunday morning and Horsford wanted a professional player. First of all we had Adams, from Cambridgeshire and his friend Green. This enabled us to hold our own in the Norfolk Alliance but the committee decided they wanted a high-profile player to keep pace with the other teams. Somehow, I had the number of Richie Richardson, captain of the West Indies. I phoned him and asked how much he would charge to play for Horsford. He said: "£20,000 plus a house, a car – and he would coach as well. This was beyond our budget.

Going in to bat with cricket stars

Champion young cricketers from Norfolk are padding up for a date with England players.

Nasser Hussain and several of his colleagues will coach Horsford under-15s on Friday prior to their winter tour to South Africa and Zimbabwe, writes Keith Peel.

The session with the stars is part of Horsford's reward for winning the prestigious Sun Life of Canada under-15 competition, which attracted more than 1500 teams from all over the country.

"It's an all-day session at Major Ronald Ferguson's indoor school in Basingstoke and will be an occasion the boys will remember all their lives," said Horsford team manager Mike Rowson.

"They also won £500 from the Lord's Taverners for a charity of their choice and this will be presented to Dereham Training Centre on October 28 by former Norfolk and Essex player Don Topley." The Lord's Taverners have also given Horsford a large bag of cricket equipment.

Picture: SUBMITTED

CHAMPIONS: Horsford players and team manager Mike Rowson (right) pictured with England players Darren Gough and Alex Tudor after winning the Sun Life of Canada national under-15 title at Basingstoke. Back (l-r): Anthony Reeve, Sean Burridge, John Sutton, Oliver Bishop, Lee Cornfield and Michael Pickett. Front: Tom Fraser, Lee Bowker, Eddie Hopkins, George Walker, Tom Henry and Alec Broom.

Article taken from the Eastern Daily Press, Tuesday, October 19, 1999
Reproduced by courtesy of Archant Publications

Catherine was doing her teaching practice at Old Buckenham School and, on a foggy night, had to drive to a parents' evening. I told her I would go and fetch her if she struggled to drive home. The phone rang at 10.45pm and I thought it was my daughter. It wasn't; it was Richie Richardson. He was on a plane, travelling to the next one-day match. He had a young player called Karl Tuckett, who would like to play in England – for £5,000. I asked how good he was and Richie said: "You got sky? He's playing against England the day after tomorrow!"

I phoned the committee and told them to watch. Karl Tuckett bowled and despatched Hick, Stewart and another big name. The committee thought he would do for Horsford!

Now, Karl Tuckett wanted to stay with a Christian family. After much negotiation he arrived at Heathrow and was picked up by Steve Read and stayed at our house for the cricket season. There were many interesting incidents during his time with us including a great conversation between Catherine and Karl when he had left his bowling boots at the house and wanted her to take them to North Runton – an hour away. She suggested he borrow some but he won and she took the boots!

As Chairman of Horsford, having given up playing, I decided to umpire for the 2nds and I did this until one day Dick Chappell phoned and asked me to umpire with him at Great Witchingham as they were an umpire short. Following this, he suggested that I take the umpire's exam. After various lectures and practical tests, I passed my level 1 umpire's exam. I then continued to Level 2 which meant that I umpired county Under-19 games – Norfolk against Essex and Northamptonshire. I also umpired numerous Norfolk Alliance games plus a number of Under 15 county games. I also went on to umpire Bliss Cup finals and Carter Plate finals. I umpired for Framlingham College and also senior ladies county games – Norfolk v. Notts and Norfolk v. Essex.

Robert Carter, who used to be in my Norfolk Under -15 side, played for Northamptonshire and ended up as senior coach. I used to scout for him and send boys to Northamptonshire. Bryan Reynolds used to come to games I was attending and look out for good players not attached to 1st class counties. When I went to Northants I was always allowed to sit in an executive box and once took my son-in-law with me. We sat in an executive box and were allowed to stay when other people were moved on. Rory was amused to think he was not 'Joe public'.

On a number of occasions I was invited into the pavilion and at one time spent an hour-and-a-half with Matthew Haydn, opening batsman for Australia. He talked about different coaching methods between Australia and England. I also talked with Andy Lloyd, who always called me 'Turks' because I came from Norfolk. I was often able to lunch with the players and on one occasion, Elizabeth and I went to a presentation lunch at Northants - and sat with Pemberthy, Sales and their wives.

Football

The first Norwich City football match I watched was in 1951 – Norwich 0, Brighton 1! Mr Kendall took us to watch Norwich v. Aldershot, which we won 4 – 3. As the years progressed, Catherine did ballet lessons in Norwich and in the afternoon I would take her to the football. Before all this, Billy Stibbons had two seats near the Directors' Box. He didn't like driving so he asked me to drive him and I had a free ticket!

When Catherine went to boarding school, Neil had her front row ticket. Then began the fun! Before every game, Norwich goalkeeper Bryan Gunn used to shake Neil's hand. There were numerous incidents with Neil in the front row. One of the most memorable was when Vinny Jones – the notorious Wimbledon player – went to take a long throw and stood in front of Neil. Neil poked him in the back and Vinny Jones turned round to scowl at him and said: "What's the matter with you?" Neil said: "I can't see, Mr Jones". So Vinny moved but the referee came over and told Vinny Jones to take the throw at the right spot. Jones pointed out that Neil couldn't see and by this time everyone was laughing. The referee said: "What do you mean, he can't see? There are 20,000 others here!" Vinny Jones was laughing so much he threw the ball to a Norwich player and said to Neil: "Now look you've made me do!"

We always got to the match early – about 1.30pm and the next year, when Wimbledon came, Vinny Jones came to see Neil and shake hands with him. On another occasion, Danny Wallace was sub and we had heard on the news about him getting fit using an exercise bike. We were trying to persuade Neil to do the same and Danny Wallace came and explained to him why it was a good idea. The Manchester United back wanted Wallace to go on but Wallace didn't hear him so they sent Denis Irwin, a prominent international player, to tell him to go on. Wallace told Irwin to stop and talk to Neil – which he did!

On another occasion, playing Arsenal, in the last added minutes, Arsenal had a throw, again in the vicinity of Neil. Dixon, Arsenal's full-back, was taking the throw and said to Neil: "This is going in". Neil said it wasn't and Ian Wright was standing in the middle yelling at Dixon not to waste time. Dixon threw the ball in but it was cleared. "I told you so," said Neil.

At the end of one season, Catherine took Neil to the football and Neilson gave him his shirt – he refused to let anyone else in the crowd take it and deliberately gave it to Neil. Craig Bellamy – one rainy night against Bolton, spent 15 minutes talking to Neil. He remembered seeing Neil shaking hands with Bryan Gunn before every game when he (Craig) was a young lad in the crowd.

On many other occasions Neil spoke to Bobby Robson, Kevin Keegan and Nigel Worthington. They all very kindly spent time with him.

We went to a few away games. At Aston Villa we got off the coach and a man in an Aston Villa blazer told us to follow him. We went up some carpeted steps and into an executive suite. Neil and I were with his school caretaker Mr Johnson and one of his fellow students, Neil Moon. I asked if Mr Johnson had set it up but he said no. The man who was accompanying us said he thought those two boys should have something special. The boys were given Cokes and sat by an enormous television. Jackie Charlton was there. A football was produced and Jackie Charlton, Ireland manager, asked if Neil was Irish. I said his grandmother was and Charlton said Neil could play for the Ireland tam! We were then given four free seats in the front row of the upper tier. Norwich lost 3-2 but we would have been embarrassed if they had won!

Something similar happened when we went away to Derby. This time, a Norwich City player gave us four tickets for the stand behind the goal.

Neil and I carried on with our support as season ticket holders at Norwich until 2013 when we realised that travelling was too much hassle, with Neil not walking so well. During some seasons, Catherine and/or Elizabeth would come too.

After we moved to Saxmundham in 2008, when Norwich were playing away we watched Leiston if they were at home. Now that we are no longer able to attend, Neil keeps up with the scores on TV and his iPad.

Catherine

Towards the end of her time at Oakham School, Cath went for university interviews and was offered a place, conditional on exam results, at Clare College, Cambridge, with a place in the College choir. This was for a year later so Cath went to France in her year out, to live with a French family and help look after the children.
In many ways this was a very useful experience but during her time at Oakham

Cath had become a vegetarian. The French, on the whole, do not have much regard for vegetarianism and Cath came home much slimmer than when she set out for France.

With the stress and hard work of college life, rehearsals, services and concerts with the choir, including trips abroad, she continued to lose weight and eventually, during her third year, she was admitted to Addenbrookes Hospital.

She had been staying at home, waiting for a bed to become available when she received a phone call saying that she could have a place that day. It was a very windy day and some lorries had been blown over on the A14 but we made it. It was a relief that at last she would have her anorexia treated but it was still very difficult to leave her on the psychiatric ward. She was not allowed to leave the ward for some time but we were allowed to visit once a week providing that Cath had gained a certain amount of weight. Gradually, over the following weeks she was allowed to visit other parts of the hospital (restaurant, shops etc) and then we could take her out for a few hours.
Cath took her final exams while still an in-patient and managed to get a 2:1 and even went to the degree ceremony from the hospital. We were so proud of her.

A while later, Cath was discharged as an in-patient but still had to live in Cambridge to visit the ward three times a week as an out-patient. Gradually these visits decreased until she was discharged altogether.

During Cath's first year at Cambridge we discovered that Neil was diabetic and he spent a few days in hospital while his insulin levels were sorted out. It seemed like quite a big deal to us but he took it all in his stride.

Soon after Cath came out of Addenbrookes I decided to retire from full-time teaching at Reepham High School. Elizabeth had a full-time post teaching at Aylsham and was waiting for an operation. Neil was also waiting for a corneal graft so we thought I would be better available to look after them and do some supply teaching when convenient. I tried short spells at other schools but most of this was done at Reepham High where it was lovely to be able to keep in touch with pupils and staff.

One thing I took up when I retired from teaching was singing with Reepham Singers. Following a bout of depression singing was a useful help, especially with an established choir. Bernard Franklin, the conductor, had been a teacher at Reepham Primary School and had encouraged Catherine in her love of singing and playing the recorder when she was a pupil there.

We did two concerts each year – carols and a summer concert with various extras in between. Once, we did The Messiah, which Dick Le Grice had to conduct as Bernard was ill, leaving Mike Fuggle and me as the only tenors. He was good at finding the right notes so I followed him and we held our own against the sopranos!

From time to time, when Cath came back to live at Reepham, she also joined the Singers and found it as helpful as I had, especially since John Taylor (a bass with the Singers) introduced her to other singers and groups.

Some of the more memorable lessons when I was on supply was when I was asked in to Reepham as a qualified teacher to sit in on talks given by visiting college lecturers to give older pupils an idea of what courses were available to them at local colleges. I had to go in early to make sure rooms and necessary equipment were ready and we had afternoon tea before commencing the talks. Subjects ranged from flower arranging, animal care, hairdressing, catering and agriculture. Even in those days I didn't have a lot of hair so the pupils found it amusing when the lecturer said she would use me as a model. Would there be time for extensions? She said she would demonstrate head massage, which proved to be very soothing. I was woken by a shout of: "Miss! Miss, he's gone to sleep!"

Another very interesting session was the animal care, when the tutor brought in a cockerel and placed it on the side near a boy who fussed and complained when asked to do some writing. Whereupon the cockerel took exception to someone outdoing him and crowed rather alarmingly. Boy was quiet! On hearing this next day, several staff requested cockerels for their classrooms!

About the same time that I had retired from full-time teaching I also gave up being Chairman of Horsford Cricket Club. Negotiations had begun regarding Norfolk County Cricket playing home matches at Horsford since Lakenham would no longer be available. It was soon clear that a chairman with more business experience than I had was needed. However, I had begun to do some umpiring for Horsford 2nd XI while Brian Broome was ill. Dick Chappell was short of an umpire and asked if I could help out. After the match he suggested I do the Level 2 umpiring course and could then officiate in the Alliance and Premier and 1st divisions.

Everybody on the course was surprised to find out how much they didn't know. We had to buy a copy of the Tom Smith Umpires' book, which contained details of all that we knew, or didn't know, about cricket. Following the written exam we had to go to Chelmsford for a practical assessment. After a while I received a letter saying that I had passed my Level 2 and I could umpire Premier League games and county games up to Under-19 level. I umpired a Bliss Cup Final and Carter Plate Finals and a 20-20 Final in front of quite large crowds.

Other memorable games were Norfolk Under-19s versus Essex Under-19s, run by Keith Fletcher and Graham Saville and also two ladies games Norfolk v. Essex and Norfolk v. Nottinghamshire, University games for UEA, Norfolk Under-19s v. Northamptonshire 20-20 with power plays etc.

In 2008, when we moved to Saxmundham I continued to go back to Norfolk to umpire (having requested south of the county) but found the travelling was more than I really wanted. I did some umpiring for Framlingham College and charity matches at Brandeston so I gave up umpiring in Norfolk.

Saxmundham Sports Cricket 1st Xl
Having won the Suffolk Cricket Alliance John Boast Memorial Plate in 2013

I wandered up to Carlton Park one Sunday afternoon to see what the cricket was like. They didn't appear to have umpires so I volunteered. Around this time I had another bout of depression so was really looking for something to do to occupy my time. The first game was with Saxmundham 2nd XI. One particular incident springs to mind. A batsman hit the ball into the covers and I sprinted into position to line myself up to adjudicate if necessary on a quick single. Nothing else happened – the batsman didn't run, the fielders didn't hurry but threw the ball back to the bowler. Steve Brett put his arm round my shoulder and we all laughed as he said: "I think you're used to umpiring something different to this!" But this was a great help to me at the time as I felt I could be of some use to them.

After a while I became chairman of the club and umpired home matches for both the 1st and 2nd teams. Neil was delighted to find that they had a board where he could put the score up at the end of each over. No electronics at Carlton Park! I continued umpiring until late summer 2014 when my eyes became troublesome.

Resurrection of football career

Article taken from the Beccles and Bungay Journal 2002?
Reproduced by courtesy of Archant Publications

Chairman of Reepham Town

I had given up playing football when I was 28 and left training college. Injuries seemed to be taking a longer recovery time and I didn't want to be carrying injuries when I was teaching PE all day.

Sometimes, when Norwich City had an away game I would watch Reepham Town and I had a couple of stints as Chairman. I once had to referee when the referee failed to turn up to the Anglian Combination game – no referee's gear, just normal clothes. This was particularly tricky when Tommy Lake dived in the penalty area – no way could I give a penalty.

What I remember most about my job as Chairman of Reepham Town was literally being the chairperson and putting out the chairs in exactly the correct positions in the Town Hall every Friday night for the fund-raising bingo sessions.

This progressed during my second stint as chairman to becoming the bingo caller, when nobody else would do it. An interesting occupation even if I did get stick for not calling the right numbers.

I said I had retired from playing but I was wrong. Someone from Dereham Day Services, which Neil attended after he had left school, rang to ask if I could help out. This was after I had retired from full-time teaching and was well into my 50s. Someone had organised a tournament for people with special needs and they hoped to send a six-a-side team from Dereham but had no footballing staff to take them. So I agreed to go. Team managers had to be part of the team.

I took my trainers and thought I would play in goal but no, managers had to play out. Managers were also not allowed to score.

The teams were not very evenly matched and for some of our players it was the first time they had been involved in a match. One of our players had new trainers for the occasion and every time he kicked the ball, had to inspect to see if his trainers had been damaged. The goalkeeper complained that the opposition were kicking the ball too hard. However, we all survived several short games.

Following this, Norwich City's Football in the Community organised several more tournaments, with teams more suitably matched and these didn't require a manager to play. David Crombie, from Dereham Day Services, took over the organisation and training and one year, Dereham won their group. I thought my involvement was over but I was wrong once again.

One day, David rang to ask if I could help him out. Dereham were to represent Norwich City at a national tournament at the David Beckham Centre in London.

I said of course I would go to help.

A little while later he rang again to say we were staying overnight – the FA were paying for us to stay in an hotel.

On arrival we were very surprised to see the hotel we were booked into – much grander than any of us expected. David gave a talk on how to use the keycards and expected behaviour. He asked me if he had forgotten anything – I suggested no-one should leave the hotel until we were ready to leave for the tournament the next day. The Docklands Light Railway was just outside our hotel and I had visions of some of our party disappearing up West!

The next day we went to the David Beckham Centre – a massive place which left several of our group awe-struck. The kit had been provided by Norwich.

A number of teams played in club kits provided by their local professional clubs. The boys enjoyed taking part but didn't manage to win a game. Neil scored in one game, to the delight of the team, but celebrated by pulling his shirt over his head, colliding with the ref and receiving a yellow card. A good time was had by all and several of the boys slept all the way back to Dereham.

I forgot to mention the last Norwich City away game that Neil and I went to. Norwich had reached the Championship play-off final to go into the Premier League. Wembley was being renovated so we had to go to Cardiff instead – but how to get there? Both train and bus would have involved long journeys with uncertain meal breaks. But then it was announced that several planes would be leaving Norwich Airport for Cardiff and back again. Following a phone call to book our tickets, I had to travel into Hellesdon, to the travel agency, with a letter from the doctor saying that Neil would need to carry diabetic needles etc and was informed that we would also need our passports on the day of travel – I might not have thought of them – some didn't!

On the day, after breakfast, we left for the airport and found lots of other people also opting for air travel. I think we took off at about half past ten and arrived at the airport at half past eleven, travelling by bus to the city centre. We walked towards the Millennium Stadium, which is near Cardiff Castle, looking for somewhere to eat lunch, when we came to a dual carriageway and Neil and I headed for an underpass. We were asked by some Birmingham supporters where we were going.

A big Birmingham lad said: "Don't go down there – you could be confronted by some Cardiff locals who are not always welcoming. Come with us and we'll get you across the dual carriageway."

I never would have tried that myself but from this group of 30 to 40 Birmingham supporters, two walked on either side of Neil and helped him along while others stopped the traffic and we just walked across a very busy road.

On the other side we met a lot of Norwich fans and a number asked if we were ok. We were still trying to find lunch and someone told us of a cafe in the Castle grounds so that's where we had our meal at about 12.30. We had enjoyed a lovely flight in clear weather with a good view of the Clifton suspension bridge.

We made our way to our seats in the stadium; I sat Neil down and went off to get him a couple of diet Cokes but when I came back two people unknown to me had bought him some already. Atomic Kitten were providing the pre-match entertainment, at least trying to, we couldn't hear them because the crowd was making so much noise with both sets of supporters singing along together. It made for a lovely atmosphere.

We scored first but eventually lost on penalties. On the way back to the coach there was very little traffic on the dual carriageway so we were able to cross on our own and came to the entrance of City Hall where I spotted John Charles, wearing a dinner jacket. In earlier times he was one of the greatest centre forwards. He shook hands with Neil and embraced him and stopped for a chat, asking if we had enjoyed the day – which we had, despite losing.

The journey home was uneventful apart from a bumpy landing at Norwich airport. In my opinion the happy experience of this day, despite losing, stood Norwich in good stead through the following seasons when, despite being relegated to Division One of the League they still maintained good crowds and strong support, rising to the Premier League again.

Trains

When I was about seven or eight (early 1950s) Mother and I moved to Melton Constable from Royston. Father had disappeared from the scene when I was about three or four and Mother had a new job as Secretary at Melton Constable

Secondary Modern School. First we rented rooms in the house of Mr Barstard (sen). I couldn't understand his broad Norfolk accent. After a while, we moved to his son Fred's home, with his wife, Olive. Fred worked on the railway.

Melton Constable village had expanded rapidly with the railway, which was a main junction from the Midlands to Norwich, one track to Sheringham and the North Norfolk coast and another, possibly to North Walsham. The rows of terraced houses resembled an industrial area, which indeed Melton Constable was. Between the wars they built engines there – they used to call it the 'miniature Crewe'.

And so began my love of railways. The train from the Midlands – the Leicester Express, was divided up with some carriages going to Norwich, some to the North Norfolk coast, involving a lot of shunting and a turntable. There was also a private platform for Lord Hastings, possibly as a result of much of the track locally going over his land.

As if all this activity wasn't enough for a young boy's imagination occasionally there would be training sessions for the railway staff, involving the use of a model railway. Fred would take me and my friend along with him where we could sit and watch, with strict instructions not to say anything.

Sometimes, in summer, Mother would collect me after school and we would go on a train to Sheringham for tea and then a game of cricket on the beach – if the tide was out.

Frequently we would travel to Bungay by train, from Melton Constable to Norwich City Station and a long walk to Thorpe Station. Sometimes we would take a taxi for the return journey. The train from Norwich Thorpe went to Tivetshall, where we changed off the main line (to Ipswich) on to the Waveney Valley line and so to Bungay where we would walk to my grandparents' house in Beccles Road – another long walk. Sometimes we would catch a bus from Norwich to Bungay.

Once, when I was staying with Granny and Grandad, Granny and I walked from their house to the common, where the swings were, crossing over the bridge across the railway line to get there. We stopped to look at an engine which was shunting trucks. We went on to the common and I played for a while, then we walked back to the fence so I could watch the engine. Granny found a seat nearby. The engine paused in its shunting near where I was standing and the driver waved and asked if I would like a ride. Would I?!

Granny said it was ok and the driver told her to collect me from the station platform later. I crawled under the wire fence and scrambled down the bank.

The fireman helped me up into the engine and sat me on a seat in the cab. Off we went to do some shunting. It was very noisy and hot and I noticed my hands were getting dirty when I touched things. After about 20 minutes they took me back to the station where Granny was waiting. We thanked the driver and fireman. I think Granny was pleased to see me but not the state I was in.

On our way home it started to rain and along our way, a lady Granny knew poked her head out of her door and said:"Come in Mrs Honeywood and wait for the rain to stop". There was no way Granny was going to take me into someone's house looking like a coal miner – so we walked home in the rain! Grandad, however, was quite envious of my adventure.

The first model railway I had was at Granny and Granddad's' - a circular track and one engine, with a tender, going round the dining room table.

Back at Melton Constable a new boy, Christopher Pill, started at school and said his family and the farm were moving on to the Study estate. I asked how they were going to do that – the whole farm. He said everything, except the house and land, would be coming up by train during the school half-term holiday. So I, of course, went to watch from the bridge with some other pals. It was an amazing sight with all the cattle, farm machinery and other equipment. Apparently they had come by rail all the way from Cornwall

Another memory of 1953 was when my mother had gone by train to Norwich leaving me to watch a football match in Melton Constable. The wind had become so strong that the goalie couldn't kick the ball out of the penalty area and the game was abandoned. I walked to the station to meet my mother off the train and as she came off the steps from the platform she was nearly blown over. This turned out to be the weekend of the great floods along the East Coast.

A few days later, when the storm and tides had receded, we went out on our bikes to look at the flooding and damage, which all along the coast and in places for several miles, was devastating.

In a book called North Sea Surge there is an account of the train in the Heacham area that was hit by a wind-blown chalet, which just caught the train's smoke stack – the train managed to stay on the tracks.

We moved to Loddon when Mother was secretary at Loddon Secondary School but the town didn't have a station. So until Mother purchased a car in 1956, we travelled by bike or bus. All holidays after that were taken in Mother's Austin.

A neighbour, Philip Kendle, had a model railway similar to mine and we put the sets together involving a crossing of the tracks. We constructed a tunnel over the crossing and the clockwork trains were wound up and set off. All went well until they met at the crossing in the tunnel. To our amazement there was a crash followed by the trains coming out of the tunnel, still on the tracks but not in the intended directions.

Many years later, when we lived at Reepham, I sold the clockwork set and bought a 00 gauge electric set. I set it up on planks round the edge of the garden but one small stretch had to cross the lawn. I dug out a bit of lawn to sink the track so I could still cut the grass. This track needed a lot of maintenance; I had to clean it every time before I ran a train on it, which took some time. Passing birds, cats and leaves were discouraged.

One summer day I came home from school and Elizabeth said: "Sit down and have a cup of tea," and I noticed she had cut the grass. "Thank you," I said. "Well done." "Not too well done," she said. "There was a bit of a problem." You've guessed it. Apparently bits of track flew in all directions in an alarming manner.

That made the decision to relocate the track, this time in the conservatory. One evening, Cath and I were operating the trains and switched off the room lights so that we could watch the 125 going round with its front and rear lights glowing. It had about six carriages, including a restaurant car. A neighbour's cat turned up and watched through the glass, becoming quite alarmed as the lights came round the bend and sped towards it, only to disappear round another bend. The cat became so upset we had to switch off the train and put the main lights on again. Having the train in the conservatory was all right in the cooler months but in summer the temperature rose so much that some of the track buckled and the restaurant car looked as if someone had overcooked the dinners!

Next location was the loft. There was plenty of floor space but I thought it would save a lot of bending if we put the shelving at waist height. Our friend Vic Lunn spent several hours organising this, for which was really thankful as my woodworking skills were not great. There was plenty of room for double track, points, sidings, stations with three platforms, crossovers etc. I spent many happy hours organising that, especially after I retired from full-time work.

When we had fund-raising coffee mornings, those who were brave enough to tackle the ladder, were allowed into the loft, but not too many at once.

There was also very useful storage space under the shelving for all the Poppy Appeal paraphernalia when we were organisers for the area.

After several years of enjoyment, the railway in the loft came to an end when we had the cavity walls filled with insulating material. There was dust everywhere over the tracks despite my attempts to cover them. Eventually I decided to sell some of the engines and rolling stock and donated the rest to Dereham Day Services which, initially, was warmly welcomed but then it was found that none of the staff had time to organise it, so gave it all back! Fortunately a new home was found for it at Whitwell Station, which had been taken over by a railway preservation society, which also had room for model railways.

Living at Reepham we were fortunate to be within easy reach of several narrow gauge railways which we visited when Cath and Neil were younger – Walsingham to Wells and another to the caravan site, the Bure Valley Line (Aylsham to Wroxham), the Barton House railway, reached by a boat trip and the Sheringham to Holt – the North Norfolk Railway.

On holidays we often seemed to find trains too, such as going up Snowdon and the Ffestiniog Railway. Eventually we found train-based holidays with Nenta Tours. At first we went on a long weekend break to Glasgow were we stayed at the Glasgow Hilton. Travelling from Norwich, a tremendous breakfast was waiting for us at Peterborough where we waited for other members of the party to join us from other directions. We then travelled north through some wonderful scenery.

Waiting for a bus next morning to take us to Loch Lomond I spotted a man with

Ordnance Survey maps of the area. "Ah," I said. "A man after my own heart." He replied that he used to teach Geography and after further discussion we realised Mr Sciveor had taught me at Wymondham College. He was pleased to find I was still using maps too.

That trip also took in a visit to the Hollow Mountain where we went on a little train to see the hydro-electric power station, which was very interesting. During the night they pumped water back to the top of the mountain ready to use to make paper when demand was high during the day and apparently this was a very profitable way of working.

We also had a train trip to Oban.

During that weekend an international bagpipe festival was held in Glasgow. The team from Ireland, who won the pipe band competition, was staying at our hotel and we chatted with them, finding out that teams from many parts of the world travelled to compete.

We saved our pennies for a longer holiday with Nenta Tours, this time taking Neil to Barcelona. He found it difficult to believe that you could get to Spain without going by boat or plane and was a bit worried by the idea of the tunnel. Soon after we left Waterloo the staff came round for breakfast orders. Neil thoroughly enjoyed his breakfast and eventually asked about the tunnel, only to be told that we were through it and were now in France.

At Lille we changed trains for Montpellier where we spent the night. In the morning we boarded a train for Barcelona and travelled through some very different countryside on the edge of the Camargue. The train stopped at the Spanish border for armed guards to board and check our passports and while this was going on, the bogies were being changed because the track gauge is different in Spain to that in France.

Eventually we went on our way but not very far – we came to an abrupt halt. Apparently there was a problem with the overhead pantograph. Fortunately, a local train came by on another track and we were told to clamber off our train – with our luggage – and climb aboard the other train. Unfortunately it was already fairly full so we and our luggage were packed in like sardines. Some students kindly offered us seats and were keen to talk to us in English because they were studying Shakespeare. We thought this a really nice welcome into Spain, or rather Catalonia, as our students insisted.

Stopping at the local halts we eventually reached Barcelona and spent a very interesting week, including a trip to Monserrat, an abbey high in the mountains where there was a festival of dance with groups from all over the local areas. We went higher up the mountain in a funicular railway, giving us a good view of the dancing in the square below.

Another day we visited Tarragona with its impressive Roman ruins and then went back to Barcelona by the scary scenic route along the cliffs.

From Barcelona, back to Montpellier we had a fairly uneventful journey but the next day from Montpellier to Paris our seats were reserved on the upper tier of a double-decker train. Walking when the train was at full speed was quite tricky as three was a fair amount of sway.

The Eurostar and Tunnel held no fears for Neil by now – he was just wondering what he would be offered to eat.

Our next holiday involving trains was actually a coach trip to Wales, where we stayed at Molde. The first train was the Welsh Highland railway from Rhydale to Carmarthen. I believe the line has now been extended from Rhydale to connect with the Ffestiniog Railway. We also went on the Bala Lake Railway.

The next trip with Nenta Trains was to Switzerland. After Eurostar we travelled through Germany, the scenic route alongside the Rhine, after our stopover in Cologne. We headed for Chur, in eastern Switzerland for the first few days. From Chur we travelled to Pontresina where it was very cold but worth going for a very picturesque journey over viaducts and round mountains. After further trips in the Chur area we boarded the Glacier Express taking us to Brig – it was an amazing train, with windows in the roof allowing fabulous panoramic views. Even in June there were icebergs floating down the rivers.

The surprising thing in Brig was the railway station where there was no fencing, crossing gates or similar safety precautions; the tracks just seemed to be part of the street, similar to trams. Pedestrians just seemed to watch out for trains and keep out of the way. The next day we went to Zermatt where we knew that at some stage

we should be able to have a trip in a horse-drawn carriage – an easy way to see quite a lot of the place and which pleased Neil no end.

You could also take a rack-and-pinion train part-way up the Matterhorn – to a restaurant of course. On the journey back down the mountain we managed to get seats right at the front, just behind the driver's cab. Once he had started us off he folded his arms as we proceeded on our way – much to Neil's alarm, but we reassured him that everything was ok.

The following day we went to Bern where we saw the usual touristy things. Other trains took us to other places in western Switzerland. Trains were invariably on time and ran like clockwork.

Heading for home we were to come back through France, catching the Eurostar in Paris. No change of train until Paris but a change of driver and guard at the Swiss/French border. Unfortunately the French driver did not turn up for over an hour so we would not make the Eurostar we had been booked on – lots of work for the tour organiser but we made it home eventually.

Our next big train trip was to Austria. Saxmundham to Salzburg, then by coach to Bad Ischl where we stayed. Bad Ischl was on a railway line but not one that connected easily to Salzburg. We had some wonderful trips out among the mountains and lakes.

A similarly scenic journey was during a cruise holiday in the Norwegian Fjords, when we left the ship at Flam and travelled by train to Voss. I think that particular train must have been mainly for tourists because we stopped at especially beautiful sites so that people could take photographs. It was a gloriously sunny day.

On a coach holiday to Scotland we stayed at Fort William and from there took a trip to Mallaig on the Jacobite Steam railway passing the Glenfinnian Viaduct and we had two hours in Mallaig before returning to Fort William. The next day we went by coach to the Kyle of Lochalsh and over the bridge to Skye for a quick look round before boarding the train which would take us through the Highlands to the east coast at Dingwall. I was in charge of the tickets for the party since the driver had to take the coach to pick us up at Dingwall.

Another steam train we enjoyed was the Strathspey Railway from Aviemore to the Boat of Garten. The coach picked us up at the Boat of Garten and as we went over the railway bridge the train passing underneath gave us a whistle. On our way back to Fort William we stopped off at the Commandos' Memorial before heading up Glen Nevis where much of the film 'Braveheart' was made.

With music from the film playing as we travelled it was a moving experience.

Meanwhile, nearer to home, we found the Mid-Suffolk Light Railway, near the Mendlesham Mast. We took our grandson, Felix, with us and Neil and discovered it was a 40s re-enactment day, very inexpensive to get in and we all enjoyed the steam train which went up and down the track for about half a mile and you could go as many times as you liked without paying any extra.

People were dressed as Capt. Mainwaring and his gang of Home Guards who took part in some kind of drill, Land Army girls, Winston Churchill and other people dressed for the times.

There was a display of assorted military vehicles of the time, which were interesting. Neil was particularly taken with a collection of armaments and the man in charge was very patient answering Neil's questions. Felix, however, was more interested in the RAF fire engine and was allowed to climb on board (with his grandmother) and the man in charge said: "Would you like a ride?" – echoes of granddad as a boy! Of course, they said: "Yes, please!" Elizabeth shouted to me that they were going for a ride and I assumed it would be out of one entrance and in by another – a quick trip round the block. Other people were getting in until the fire engine had a full crew. Elizabeth sat in the front seat with Felix on her knee and off they went.

About 20 minutes later they still had not come back and I was beginning to get a bit anxious. When eventually they turned up they told us they had been parked on Mendlesham Airfield while the driver answered questions, such as where did he get spare parts.

There was a nice restaurant and a museum as part of the set-up. During the year they had various open days, some with themes, and you could go to any of them on your original ticket – what good value.

While we were there I purchased an N-gauge horsebox, which leads me on to my

N-gauge model railway. When we moved to 53 Heron Road we had a tandem garage but only one car. That car I managed to park in the garage, leaving half of it unoccupied except for the tumble drier and a few other spare items, tins of paint, flower pots etc, which left plenty of room for a waist-level base board for a railway. As you may remember, my carpentry skills were not great but I had made another carpenter friend, Paul Golding, who constructed it as required.

So I set about designing an N-gauge railway. During the winter I designed the city collage and various other scenes as background. On every visit to Lowestoft my steps took me to Parr's model railway shop and I gradually accumulated track and kits for making stations etc.
After Felix was born we changed to a larger car in order to transport buggy and other equipment and unfortunately I couldn't park it in the garage. What should we do with the extra space? Call on Paul Golding again to enlarge the base board, so now we had a dockland area too.

Eventually the set-up had a terminus at one end and the docks at the other so a train could go all the way round and there were also local lines and a heritage line. Felix enjoyed sharing it with me and I was pleased to show anyone interested. Sometimes, when we had coffee evenings, the trains would feature as an attraction although it was rather cold out in the garage in winter.

Church

Although I have mentioned church in previous chapters because, of course, church and religion should not be separate from the rest of your life, I think it deserves and chapter of its own, to fill in the gaps.

I have the odd recollection of a church visit when we lived in London. The first time I really remember going was to the church in Melton Park. We sat near the back and were almost the last out because we were having a look round when a man came up and said: "Have a better look round my church." This turned out to be Lord Hastings. I went up some steps and mother called me back. Lord Hastings said: "Oh, that's all right, he can go into my box".

On another occasion I was in the congregation sitting behind two ladies. One of them didn't have a hymn book. We had a spare one so I poked her in the back with the hymn book. She turned round and smiled and said: "Thank you". No more was said but when mother was at school on the Monday she asked who the two ladies were and was told that the one I had poked in the back was the Duchess of Beaufort!

We often used to cycle through the park and when I saw the two ladies again I shouted: "Wotcher!" to be severely reprimanded by my mother. Next time I saw them I raised my cap.

After a while, Mrs Drury, who lived next door, persuaded us to go to Burgh Parva Church which was nearer and had a corrugated iron roof – the old church was in ruins next door. I could sing quite well so was asked to join the choir and we went there for the rest of the time we were at Melton Constable.

We then moved to Loddon and I once again joined the choir. There were regular practices and I was encouraged by Mr and Mrs Spurgeon. They gave me a watch because I kept asking them the time. On a number of occasions I was asked to sing the first verse of 'Once in Royal David's City' at Christmas-time which I thought was a great honour. I also carried the cross.

Later on, when the choir had a particularly enthusiastic choirmaster, as well as the church music we put on performances of Stainer's 'Crucifixion', Handel's 'Messiah' and even 'Hiawatha's Wedding Feast' and Gilbert and Sullivan's 'Trial by Jury'.

By this time I was in the RAF and couldn't always be around for practices, services and concerts but Elizabeth had joined the choir by then, with others from Sisland Church, which was part of the benefice, which was how we got to know each other. I carried on going to church at Loddon and Sisland when I had a weekend off from the RAF and in holiday times.

I've already told you something of the church life in Singapore when I was stationed there. The George Club was connected to the church, they had a drama group that I belonged to and an Anglican Young People's Association, of which I became chairman.

On some special occasions, we went to Singapore Cathedral, which had been built by Indian convicts. In the Cathedral grounds there were snake charmers and I have a photo of me wearing a snake as a scarf!

The architecture of the Cathedral was similar to what you might expect in England, except for the fans. The brickwork was white and very clean, probably due to the fact that there were no manufacturing industries there, at least, not in the 1960s. It seemed strange singing Christmas carols in that heat but I don't remember doing 'In the Bleak Midwinter' or similar.

Each RAF station on the island held a church fete every year, attended by hundreds of people, raising money for charities, not the upkeep of the church, and we all went to visit each other's event.

When I returned from Singapore in January 1968 I went back to worshipping at Loddon and Sisland churches. Although I was stationed at Coltishall I usually had weekends off work. After Elizabeth and I were married, in July 1968, we went to live at Horstead and worshipped there, singing in the choir, as I have already mentioned in an earlier chapter. After a couple of years I became a member of the Parochial Church Council and then was churchwarden. Some of the Deanery meetings were held at Blickling Hall, which made a change from the usual church halls.

During my time at Horsford I played a few times for the Diocesan cricket and hockey teams. The Bishop of Norwich himself played for the hockey XI and the cricket team was umpired by the Bishop of Lynn, the Rev. Aubrey Aitken (also a staunch Norwich City supporter). I was in the teams because our vicar, John Towler asked me to play when he was playing. He was wicket keeper for the cricket team and in goal for the hockey team. On one occasion I expressed my displeasure when John dropped a catch off my bowling, another vicar asked if I was John's curate. When I told him I wasn't, he said: "No, I thought not!"

The vicar, I later learned, was Paul Kelly, from Reepham, which of course was our next parish after we moved from Horstead.

I've found it quite difficult to put my thoughts into separate categories because there is such an overlap of subjects, particularly religion, because of course it involves all aspects of your life. For instance, the Rev. John Towler was quite pleased when we had an early service at church on a Sunday, leaving him free to play cricket for Overstrand in the afternoon. On a fine afternoon his wife and children could go and play on the beach.

We soon met up with Paul Kelly again when we moved to Reepham. I sang with the choir and after a while became a member of the PCC and eventually churchwarden. This spell as warden didn't last many years as I became too busy with work and boys' cricket, taking me away from home, to do a really good job.

One memorable churchwarden's swearing in took place in a fairly small village church in the Ingworth Deanery. The vicar of Reepham was on holiday so the churchwardens of the benefice went along without him to be sworn in. The pews were very crowded. A small man on his own was sent to join our pew so we squashed up to let him in. When our turn came to stand up to show our presence this little man stood up with us. Once we had sat down again I asked him why he had stood up with our benefice. He said: "I had no choice; when you stood up, I had to, too!" When it came to his turn we helped him up.

During the time that I wasn't churchwarden, for a few years we ran a church youth group which mainly met at our house on a Sunday evening. This was generally of a social/recreational nature but with some church-based activities and discussion. They decided to raise money for Tear Fund by washing cars on a Saturday morning. Someone from the Parish Council must have known of this because when they couldn't find anyone to clean the Market Place, they asked if our group could do very early on a Saturday morning, which some of the youngsters agreed to do. This lasted a few months. There weren't many people about at that time of day but one person we didn't expect to see was the actor who played 'Yosser' from 'Boys from the Black Stuff', who commended us on our efforts.

One year we took the group to Queen Ethelburga's School, near Harrogate for a Christian Youth Week where we learned lots of new songs and dramas to take back to Reepham.

Another activity was carol singing to elderly folk or people on their own and instead of collecting money we would take a gift. We did this for a few years but it came to a halt once people became very nervous about opening their doors at night.

Southwold Expedition

The following account of the Southwold Expedition is not memoirs, but a copy of the account Mike wrote at the time, as part of his P.E course at Keswick Hall, Norwich where he did his teacher training.

It was one of his happier memories of college life and often referred to, especially when we came to live nearer Southwold.

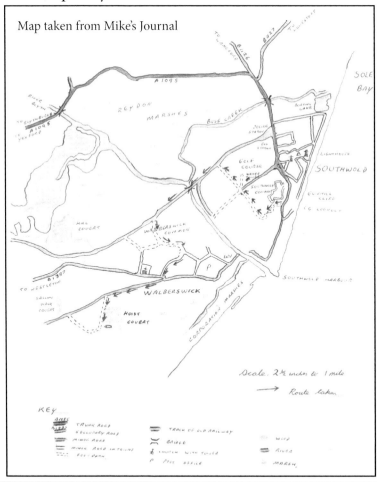

Map taken from Mike's Journal

Year One - Expedition to Southwold, Walberswick, Dunwich and Blythburgh. February 25th to 27th.

Comprising

Planning and organising the expedition

Log of the expedition

History of the surrounding area

Series of appendices

Planning and organisation

Two group discussions were held before deciding to take the Southwold area for our walk. Two areas were put forward, the other being the North Norfolk Coast but as most of the group had already been there it was decided to go to Southwold.

The group consisted of Janet Walker, Pam Watson, Joy Menage, Leslie Carter, Jerry Ricketts, Roger Cawdron, Glen Turner and myself. It was decided that Leslie should be in charge of getting the kit organised and that Glen should be the treasurer. Two cars would be used to get us to the starting point, those of Jerry and Roger. Before finalising arrangements the whole idea and route was presented to Mr Aspland, who gave us the go-ahead providing we could obtain permission for being away from college from midday Wednesday February 25th to midday Friday 27th. The reason why the Southwold-Walberswick route was chosen was because we thought that good areas for camping could be found and this proved to be the case.

On Monday February 23rd Leslie obtained the necessary kit and equipment from Mr Aspland. Four tents were used and four Primus stoves, as well as a rucksack each, plates, mugs, cutlery, tin opener, two compasses, billies and two collapsible water bottles. This kit was shared out between us.

Glen collected £1 from each of us and bought the food on Tuesday and managed to pile this all into his rucksack – as well as his own kit. This proved rather a burden for him on the first day!

Log of the Expedition

We left college at 14.00 hrs on February 25th after managing to get everything including ourselves, into the two cars and arrived at Southwold Police Station at 15.00 hrs. Here, Roger and Jerry asked the police for the best place to leave their cars. They were told to leave them at the edge of the Common and that the police would keep an eye on them. This, in fact, was an official car park.

Time	Grid ref	Observations
15.15	507760	Put our rucksacks on our backs and set off across Southwold Common, heading for the water tower. The sun was shining and the weather had provided us with a good start. We passed the water tower and then reached the golf club.
15.25	502762	From here we walked to the track of the old narrow gauge Southwold Railway which is now Tarmacked over, and crossed the River Blyth by the Bailey bridge which was built in place of the Old railway swing bridge.
15.35	495758	After crossing the bridge we walked a little further on the made-up track and then turned left and walked across Walberswick Common into Walberswick. We crossed the B1387 and proceeded through Walberswick on a minor road, in a south-westerly direction. On the way, Jerry Ricketts and I obtained water from a nearby bungalow and it was discovered one of the water bottle leaked. After getting the water, it was decided to make camp for the night at the next convenient spot. We were now walking along an unfenced oad and saw a likely spot on the left-hand side.
16.30	483742	We walked down a track for a small distance and came across Hoist Covert and decided to camp on

the edge of the covert. Tents were pitched and the evening meal soon prepared and eaten. Glen was particularly pleased to call a halt as his rucksack was feeling very heavy. By the time we had finished the meal and tidied up it was getting quite cold so it was decided we should walk back into Walberswick and spend the evening in a pub and also stock up with water supplies.

19.00	496747	We had a stroll through Walberswick which is a charming village and ended up at the village pub, where we spent an enjoyable evening singing folksongs and playing cards. Some refreshment was consumed.
23.00	483742	We left the pub at 10.30 and walked back to camp, ending The evening with a hot drink. By now it was really cold and I climbed into my sleeping bag with just about every pullover available and a tracksuit over the lot.

Thursday February 26th

08.30	483742	After having quite a good night's sleep I found myself being the first person up so got the kettle going and woke up the rest. The sun was again shining and we had a clear, blue sky – good weather for February. We had breakfast and then
10.45	483742	struck camp, tidied up the site, loaded up and proceeded in a south-westerly direction. Glen appeared to be in difficulties with his rucksack again so I changed his with mine. He soon appeared to be much more comfortable.
11.10	464737	As we came to a place called Westwood Lodge we met two farm labourers loading salt on to a wagon. We had a good chat with them and during the

course of it we were told the football results and why Norwich and Ipswich were not doing well this season. "Never did have a centre-forward, either team," was the quote.

The walk now was very pleasing, going through bracken and fern and very soon we reached the main road. Here we rested and a bite of chocolate.

11.40	451725	This road was the B1125 from Blythburgh to Westleton and we found that the walks we had been on were called Newdelight Walks. After a brief rest we started off again in the direction of Dunwich, on a minor road passing through trees belonging to the Forestry Commission.
12.00	461716	On the way we passed the fire risk warning gauge, thankfully pointing at normal for the rest of the day. After leaving the forest we walked down a slight incline and came to Bridge Farm and just further on we arrived at Dunwich Church.
12.25	475706	From here we could see Southwold Lighthouse visible in a north-easterly direction across the marshes. We went into the church and had a look round, paying particular attention to the Leper Chapel in the churchyard. Leaving the churchyard we walked up the road and into the
12.40	477706	pub at Dunwich – The Ship – where we stopped for lunch, where a good plate of sausage and chips could be had for three shillings. We also spent time planning the route ahead after a discussion with one of the locals.
13.50		We stayed there for just under the hour and then started off again, deciding to walk along the cliffs to the rear of the ruins of Dunwich Abbey. Once on top of the cliffs the view was marvellous and

14.10	478702	Southwold and the coast along Sole Bay could be seen very clearly. While we were walking around on top of the cliffs, Roger and Glen obtained provisions from the local shop and caught us up as we walked along a wooded path on the way to 'Greyfriars', which is still used by monks today. This turned out to be a collection of houses around a large hall and we soon found that we were walking along a road where no cars were allowed. On joining the main road, we followed it for a few yards before turning left and walking through a copse, to come out on a minor road which ran to Minsmere, a bird sanctuary run by the National Trust.
	475695	At this point we had a discussion as to how to proceed from here to Westleton Heath and it was decided to follow the path around Westleton
15.05	493695	Nature Reserve. We followed this for some distance in a north-westerly direction and then came across a track which we followed until we came to a minor road leading to Westleton. We walked up a slight incline and Roger and I shared one of the girls' packs between us as they were beginning to feel a bit weary.
15.25	448696	At this point we turned right, walking in a northerly direction along a track until we arrived
15.35	449700	at the B1125, the road to Blythburgh. We crossed the road and walked along a track towards Hinton High Poplars. By now, sun was shining brightly when only a few moments before it had been hailing. The walk along the track was quite hard as it was muddy and wet and in places we had to walk along the edges of ploughed fields.
15.40	444706	We crossed a minor road and walked on to Hinton

High Poplars and then to Hinton Corner where we sat down for a rest and a bite of chocolate. At this moment, morale seemed to be rather low as people were complaining of sore feet and that the pace was too fast. However, it was decided to press on as fast as possible as we wanted to make camp by at least 17.30 hrs and did not want to leave many miles to walk on the next morning. As we were leaving our rest, a postman came to collect mail at the postbox and remarked that had never seen so many people at Hinton Corner at one time.

From here we carried along a minor road, known as Hinton Walks and on arriving at the B1125 again, turned left and walked along another minor road in a north-westerly direction arriving at Pipers Farm

16.20	443733	At this point the party was well spaced out and as we had to turn right off the road again we had to wait for the rest to catch up. Once we were all together again we pressed on, walking through
16.30	445734	Hinton Lodge Farm, which had a large duck pond to the right of the road. I stopped to look at some of the birds on the water and had a chat with the farmer, who said that they often had unusual species on the pond at odd times, most likely having come from the bird sanctuary nearby.
16.40	446744	I then caught up with the rest of the party who had reached the B1387 and had turned right heading for the junction with the B1125. At the junction we had another rest – these rests seemed to be coming
16.50	454743	more frequently now. There was a discussion at this point as to which way we would proceed to Mill Covert, where we decided we would camp. After a lively discussion it was decided to walk along the
17.00	454749	B1125 to Blythburgh. This we did and turned right

down a footpath just as we got to the outskirts of Blythburgh. Here, Glen went into the village to get bread so we waited for him. When he got back it turned out that he had bought the last large loaf available in the village which was, in fact, ordered by the local constable. As luck would have it, he was in the shop at the time and let Glen have it, saying he had enough at his house.

We started off again, walking along the footpath, which was quite muddy. We were now walking on part of the track where the old Southwold railway used to run.

17.20	453753	This part of the run was called the Heronry but none could be seen at this time. We carried on along the footpath which had left the old track way and came upon a built-up path. To the left there
17.35	467748	was a small covert and it was decided to camp there. The tents were put up and a meal was soon prepared. However it was getting very cold indeed by now after the lovely hail we had had.
19.00		After the meal the rest of the party huddled in one tent while Roger and I started off back to Blythburgh to get some water, which we needed for the rest of the stay. We took the footpath but found that parts of it were impassable as the tide had come in and water had begun to fill up some of the dips. We doubled back and took a footpath round a ploughed field. It was now dark so we had a bit of a job as the torch we had was not so good. The footpath brought us onto the B1387, which we walked along and then at the junction with the B1125 turned right and walked into Blythburgh.
20.00	453753	We immediately went into the White Hart, a lovely pub with roaring fires going at both ends of the room. A large cold buffet could be obtained but

the prices were quite high. Most people at the pub had come out from Southwold for the evening and the place seemed to be used frequently by the Southwold Rugby Club judging by the number of photographs round the place. We looked out of place with muddy boots and camping clobber on and with water bottle and kettle in hand. However, they supplied us with water and other refreshment and we sat by the lovely fire.

As soon as the publican realised that we were camping he offered us blankets and said we could sleep by the fire for the night. It was very tempting but we declined the offer as we had to get back to the others with the water.

21.00	453753	We left the pub and walked back the way we had come, arriving to find everyone huddled together keeping warm. We made hot drinks and then
22.00		crawled into our sleeping bags. I was quite tired and soon got off to sleep – again with everything on that I could find.

Friday February 27th

08.00		We woke up to find that there had been a slight snowfall and it was again very cold. Breakfast was soon in progress and after this we got the tents down and tidied up the camp site. The local gamekeeper came over and had a word telling us the quickest way to get to Southwold. He seemed rather keen that we should move on. This we did and walked on to the B1387 until we got to
10.30	471748	Eastwood Lodge Farm and here we turned left
10.45	479748	off the road and walked along the track of the old railway again and crossed the river Blyth by the bailey bridge. At this point it was snowing and

bailey bridge. At this point it was snowing and hailing and the whole area seemed very bleak. It was not at all like the first time we crossed the bridge when the sun was shining and there was a clear blue sky. We walked along the Tarmac path until we came to the old embankment where we turned right past the golf club and walked across Southwold Common to the parked cars. By this time the sun had come out again and we finished

11.30   507760   the walk in fine weather. By now the party was strung out across the common. However, we all made it and clambered into the cars and set off for college, looking forward to a nice, hot bath!

Supplies

Provisions bought by Glen before the strat:

Dried peas	2 doz. eggs	pepper
Dried green beans	2Ibs bacon	salt
Baked beans	1Ib butter	sugar
Tomatoes	1Ib cheese	tea
4 packets instant potato	cooking oil	soups
2 tins fruit cocktail	4oz coffee	drinking chocolate
8 bars of chocolate	2 packets Ready Brek	

At Southwold bread, sausages and 4 pints of milk were bought.

At Dunwich, fish fingers and milk and at Blythburgh, bread and 1Ib butter.

Menus

Wednesday evening

Soup
Sausages, potatoes and baked beans
Fruit cocktail
Bread and cheese
coffee

Thursday breakfast

Porridge
Egg and bacon
Coffee

Thursday lunch

Sausage and chips at The Ship, Dunwich

Thursday evening

Soup
Fish fingers, potatoes and peas
coffee

Friday breakfast

Boiled egg, bacon and tomatoes
Coffee

Costing

The total cost of the food amounted to £7 19s 8d, which left 4d in the kitty.

Personal equipment

My personal kit comprised a sleeping bag, anorak, two pairs of socks, two sets of underwear, two shirts, two sweaters, tracksuit, woolly hat, gloves, soap, toothbrush and towel. I wore a pair of lightweight trousers and a pair of heavy boots. The extra sweaters and tracksuit were used in the evening when it was so cold. My woolly hat kept my head warm at night. My boots were ideal for walking and I did not experience any blisters, although my feet were quite tired at the end of it all.

Camping Kit

All the tents were in excellent condition and we had no trouble at all with them but in fact the weather was very kind to us. The Primus stoves caused a bit of trouble but no doubt we were not using them right at times.

Assessment of the expedition

I enjoyed the expedition and thought the walk was most interesting. However . I do feel that we should have gone further on the first day as we had to do too much on the second to leave a short walk on the Friday morning.

Southwold

Though Southwold is a small town with a population of just over 2,000 (2,180 according to the AA members' handbook 1969!) it has a long history. It was made a Town Corporate by Charter of Henry VII and the king is commemorated in the Town Hall council chamber, by an old engraving and also by a photograph of the head of the effigy in the crypt of Westminster Abbey.

When the Charter was received, the office of Bailiff was created and in 1490 one of the bailiffs was William Godell who bequeathed to Southwold in 1506 the open space of the common. That same charter also laid down that a three-day fair could be held annually, on and after Trinity Monday, and Trinity Fair is still duly held on South Green. I used to visit the fair myself when staying at Bungay with my grandparents. The fair is formally proclaimed and opened by the Mayor, Corporation and Borough officials and custom has it that after the formal proclamation of "Oyez" etc declaimed by the Town Crier in his official hat and dress, the Mayor and others have the first ride on the merry-go-round and then adjourn to the Trinity Fair luncheon.

As we passed the Town Hall on the first day of our expedition (we were buying provisions) the rest of the party noticed that an announcement had been put up in the window asking for applicants for the post of Town Crier. They all suggested that I should put my name forward. Can't think why!

Around the Market Place stand houses of all dates, one or two said to be Tudor, others Georgian and beneath the Town Hall you can get glimpses through the gratings in the pavement of the old prison cells. The pump in the middle of the Market Place is real and until recently water could still be drawn from it. On certain days, stalls are set up round the Market Place, there by virtue of an old charter giving them the right to do so. To the right of the Market Place is a shop with large windows and I remember that for a week after the Queen's Coronation in 1953 the robes worn by the Earl of Stradbroke and his wife at the ceremony, were displayed there.

The town is unspoilt and this is partly due to the fact that Southwold is almost an island. It is surrounded by the River Blyth, the Buss creek, so called from the 'busses' or ships that once sailed there, and by the marshes. The marshlands cannot be built on; neither can the common which stretches over to Walberswick in one direction and to St Felix School in the other. The common is beautiful in spring and summer with gorse and there are plenty of walks by the reed beds and marsh meadows which adjoin the River Blyth. Sometimes you can see beautiful sunsets across the common.

There are no fewer than nine greens in Southwold. Some are said to have originated from the fire of 1659, commemorated by a plaque on the Town Hall. Many houses were destroyed and some of the greens may show where houses once stood, but others, such as South Green, have clearly been open spaces from distant times. Each green is named:

South Green; North Green; East Green; St. James's Green; Bartholomew Green; Barnaby Green and St Edmund's Green. The latter was formerly called Tibbys Green for it was once reserved for calves, or tibbys, until they were old enough to be put onto the common. Two other greens are Skilmans Hill and Gun Hill, which slopes up from South Green to the cliff. Gun Hill takes its name from the six guns that have stood there since `1745, when the Corporation petitioned King George II for means to defend the town against raiders and possible invasion. However, the guns are older than that, dating from the reign of Elizabeth I and have the Tudor badge of the Rose and Crown. They are 18 pounder culverins, old muzzle-loading guns and tradition says they were sent by the Duke of Cumberland. He may have landed at Southwold on his way from Flanders, when he was summoned back from the foreign war to deal with the Jacobite rebellion.

In 1842 they were fired as a loyal salute in honour of the Prince of Wales but, corroded by disuse, one charge exploded in the core, killing a James Martin. In the 1914-18 War, the Germans considered that these guns made Southwold a 'fortified place' and consequently shelled the town from the sea. In the 1939-45 War the guns were dismantled and hidden. They were brought from their hiding place and mounted on concrete after the war but it was not until 1959 that proper wooden copies of the originals were finally obtained and the guns correctly mounted.

Southwold suffered a good deal during the 1939-45 War. Bombs fell, one notably wiping out a row of cottages near the church and several lives were lost. Southwold itself was a 'prohibited area'. Many of its inhabitants were obliged to leave, shops were closed and boarded up and the whole town became very battered and shabby. However, it is now back to its original state and many of the old cottages have been repaired and painted. As has the lighthouse, which stands among buildings and overlooks the sea and Sole Bay.

Sole Bay was the scene of a great sea battle between the English and the Dutch on May Day 1672. From the cliffs running from Gun Hill right along the sea front, men and women watched the battle. James, Duke of York, brother of Charles II was Lord High Admiral England and had his headquarters at Southwold. James occupied an old Elizabethan house in the High Street, now called Sutherland House – now a good restaurant.

The battle raged all day. The Dutch admiral de Ruyte took James by surprise. The Earl of Sandwich, who had warned James, put to sea with his squadron while James struggled to get his own squadron to sea. Sandwich was killed and the English flagship the Royal James was lost. The Dutch fleet claimed a victory in view of the heavy casualties inflicted on the English. However, as night fell they went back to Holland and did not return. Southwold had to take charge of the wounded and the bill for nursing these men and the charge for prisoners of war came to £2,000, a bill which Charles II never paid.

Cannon balls are still occasionally dug up in Southwold gardens and coins have been found from that period, probably fallen from the pockets of those who came into the town to watch the battle. Their anxiety was heightened, no doubt, by the fact that orders had been given to break down the bridge across Buss Creek, which is still the only exit from the town, so that the countrymen who had swarmed in should be obliged to stay and help beat off a possible landing by the Dutchmen.

A museum in the town is called the Dutch Cottage. A complete panorama of the drawings of Van de Velde, of the Battle of Sole Bay, has been given and installed there and there are many local exhibits and species of birds frequenting the Southwold district. The town sign portrays an incident during the Battle of Sole Bay, where the Royal Prince, commanded by the Duke of York, is seen attacking de Ruyte's flagship De Sevin Provincien. Outside several houses can be found gaily painted ships' figureheads.

Southwold has a very large church which was built in 1460 on the site of an earlier church which was destroyed by fire. The tower is 100ft high and has many flint decorations, notably the inscription over the west door, an invocation to St Edmund "S.A.T. EDMUND ORO PRO NOBIS" and each letter being crowned. The interior flint work has been in part restored and the flints still come, as they have for centuries, from the prehistoric flint mines at Brandon – Grimes Graves. Inside is a painted mediaeval screen which stretches right across the church.

There is also a model lifeboat commemorating the days when Southwold had its own vessel. There is also a wooden figure of a Jack in armour which holds a short axe and strikes its bell before a service.

All the stained glass windows were destroyed in the 1939-45 War except the West Window. On October 26th 1954 the new East Window was unveiled by the Princess Royal.

In olden times, fishing and boatbuilding were the staple industries of Southwold. In 1839 it was recorded that 400 vessels arrived at or sailed from Southwold Harbour. In 1906 the Corporation sold the harbour to a firm of contractors who hoped to compete with Lowestoft and Yarmouth for the fishing trade from Scotland. This scheme failed and the harbour reverted to the Corporation in 1933. In 1963 an extensive repair scheme was started, costing about £110,000, however, big ships are no longer able to use the harbour because of the build up of a sand spit at the entrance. Recently there was a programme on TV, predicting that the harbour would soon be silted up forever.

The main industry of the town nowadays is, of course, tourism, and £95,000 has been spent on sea defences and improvements. Among other industries are the Dorlux Mills (bedding), Adnams Brewery and an electrical fitments factory.

The Southwold Railway

THE SOUTHWOLD RAILWAY

FURTHER to the letter in your February issue I enclose a photograph of the van in question, which has been secured for the Southwold Museum and has been removed from Halesworth to a temporary resting place beside the old booking office in the Southwold railway yard. Some expense has already been incurred and a fund has been opened to receive donations which will be used to preserve this only remaining piece of rolling stock. Donations will be gratefully received by Miss F. Foster, Treasurer for the Museum, 27 Park Lane, Southwold.

Article taken from the East Anglian Magazine April 1964

The main line of the old Great Eastern Railway had to take an inland course for geographical reasons, so the nearest station to Southwold was Halesworth, about nine miles inlands. A group of men decided to form the Southwold Railway, a private company. In 1876 an Act of Parliament was passed incorporating the Southwold Railway, authorising the construction of a line between Halesworth and Southwold, eight miles and 63 chains in length. There were to be two short branches, one to the River Blyth Navigation Quay at Halesworth and the other to the Blackshore Quay at Southwold Harbour. This would bring the total length to nine-and-a-half miles.

Construction of the line began on May 3rd 1978 and the gauge was 3ft – the only one of its kind in England. The rails were flat-bottomed, 21ft long weighing 30lbs per yard and were laid on sleepers 6in. by 3in. by 6ft long. These can still be found around Southwold. The station platforms were on the south side of the line and were only a few inches high. The line was single throughout its length with the exception of a passing place at Blythburgh and the steepest incline was 1 in 53. I all there were 13 bridges including the swing bridge over the River Blyth at Blackshore. The line was open for public traffic on September 24th 1879 following an inspection the previous day. Normal times for the trains leaving Southwold were 7.25 am, 10.05 am, 2.30pm and 5.25pm. Arrivals were at 9.17am, 1.42pm, 4.17pm and 7.02pm. Each journey took approximately 37 minutes.

The Southwold Railway had a book of rules which was strictly adhered to. Rule 92 states: "No train shall be run at a greater speed than 16 mph and the engine driver liable to two years imprisonment if convicted of doing so." Telephonic communication was maintained between the stations, the signals being lowered on receipt of advice that the train had left the previous station. Uniforms were worn, of blue serge with plain brass buttons and the letters 'SR' on the lapels and caps. The engine drivers were allowed two suits of dungarees and two caps each year and a greatcoat every three years.

The rolling stock consisted of three engines, six six-wheeled carriages, 12 open four-wheeled trucks and two four-wheeled closed wagons. One of these still remains and can be seen in Southwold Museum. The rest have long since disappeared. This remaining truck was found on an allotment at Halesworth in 1962 – being used as a garden shed.

Of the three engines, one was kept at Halesworth in case of flood which would stop through traffic, one was in regular use at Southwold and the third was used as a spare. They were originally painted green, then changed to blue with red lining and finally, black. As the railway was not equipped with a turntable, it was necessary for the locomotives to work in reverse on alternate journeys.

The seats of the passenger carriages were made of wood, covered with a strip of carpet. Two of the carriages comprised first and third class, the only difference being that first-class passengers were provided with blue cushions and separated from third class by a door. These carriages were painted a dull red with white lettering and were lit by oil lamps. One imagines that when coming towards you, the whole train would look a colourful sight.

The Southwold Railway started at Halesworth, where it had a platform of its own and its own small waiting room and office. From there it ran parallel to the main line for a few hundred yards then crossed the Southwold Road by gird er bridge and headed for the coast following the course of the River Blyth. It passed the village of Holton St Peter, going over and under small bridges crossing the river just before Blyford Hall and then entering Wenhaston Station. On this part of the journey, paper boys would be sorting their deliveries and when passing remote farms, would throw the orders out. At one place, a farmer had taught his dog to collect the papers and take them home.

One leaving Wenhaston the train continued close to the River Blyth and on approaching Blythburgh took a long curve on the outer rail, tilting the carriages at an alarming angle for the passengers. On rounding the bend the church came into view and the train passed almost under the tower and thence into Blythburgh Station. This was situated next to the London-Lowestoft road the A12, which passed over the rail by girder bridge. From here it ran by the side of the wide estuary flats and amid the tall pine trees where herons rested – and still do. This is where we camped on the Thursday night.

From the Heronry the line passed Eastwood Lodge Farm and then into Walberswick Station, which was on the common about half a mile from the village. The last part of the journey was over Tinkers Marsh to the swing bridge and thence across Southwold Common and into the station, situated on the main road into town.

In 1929 the line was closed due to financial difficulties and the last train left Southwold on April 11th of that year. The following was from an unidentified paper.

> **"Southwold's Railway's gone to pot,**
> **Where it was it now is not**
> **No good making any fuss**
> **Come to Ipswich – take a bus**
> **Southwold lies in isolation;**
> **Though they have a railway station;**
> **But, alas, no trains will run –**
> **Lookers-on enjoy the fun.**

There are still plenty of reminders of the Southwold Railway. The narrow-gauge station at Halesworth is now a coal yard although the footbridge to it has been dismantled. Some of the rail is still visible in parts although most of it is taken up, however the route is clearly traceable throughout. The site of Wenhaston station is identified by a nearby letter box of that name but only the foundations of the station remain. The Blythburgh church curve is well marked but the road bridge was removed and filled in. The concrete foundations of Walberswick station remain and from here to Southwold the track is covered by Tarmac. It used to cross the River Blyth by swing bridge but a Bailey bridge was built in its place in 1947. Where Southwold station used to be now stands the police station – the first place we went to on our expedition.

I have spoken to a number of friends of my grandparents who travelled on the Southwold Railway and my mother, too, remembered travelling on it when she was a small girl.

Another side of historical interest along our route was the small village of Dunwich which now has only a few buildings left but which once was a large place and perhaps the capital city of East Anglia. It was, in fact, the seat of the Bishopric and a thriving sea port with busy streets and markets. Coastal erosion was the cause of its decline and only the ruins of the Abbey remain. However, you can still see the outer wall and the gateway from the main road.

Dunwich also has a small museum which I believe is interesting, although I have not been inside myself. Apparently there used to be more than a dozen churches but there is only one now, built well inland although the rate at which the sea erosion is taking place perhaps even this will not be safe. Who can tell? Practically the whole village was put up for auction in 1947, when most of the tenants bought their houses and the vendor gave All Saints' Churchyard, the Reading Room and the Museum building to the Dunwich Trust to save them from ruin and desecration. The village school was also bought.

The area to the south of Dunwich is used as a bird sanctuary and is visited by many naturalists during the course of a year.

The Southwold district is certainly very interesting historically – but better visited in warmer weather!

1965

Feeding the wildlife at Thorpeness

Felix and Grandad

Cath, Felix and Rory

Respects paid to Mike – the man who made a difference

St John's Work Party

above:- PLANNING !
left :-   ACTION !
below :- POSING !

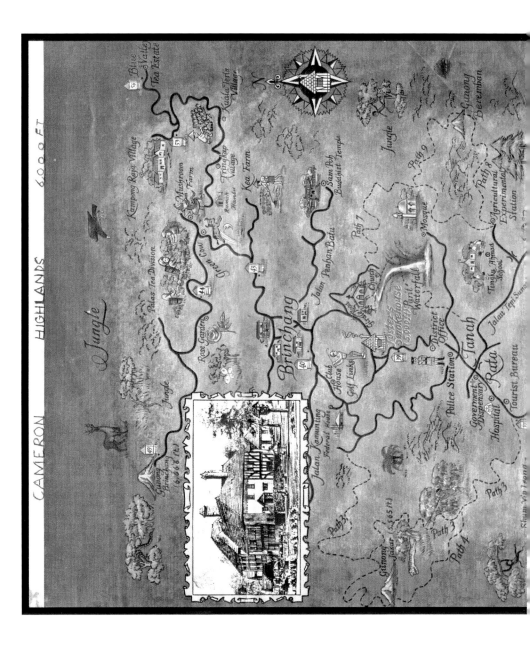

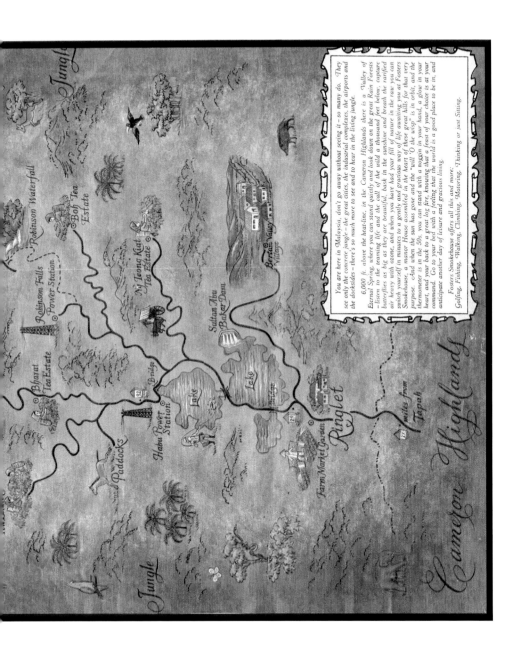

You are here in Malaysia, don't go away without seeing it – so many do. They see only the concrete jungle – the great cities, the industrial complexes, the airports and the docksides – there's so much more to see and to hear in the living jungle.

6,000 ft. above the heat-line, in the Cameron Highlands there is a Valley of Eternal Spring, where you can stand quietly and look down on the great Rain Forests – listen to the teeming life, and the call of the wild down a thousand feet below; capture butterflies as big as they are beautiful, bask in the sunshine and breath the rarified air heavy with come, then, when you have had your fill of nature in the raw you can switch yourself in minutes to a gently and gracious way of life awaiting you at Fosters Smokehouse, a manor House assembled in the heart of these great hills for that very purpose. And when the sun has gone and the "will 'O the wisp" is in orbit, and the thermometer is in the 50s you can stand with a noggin in your hand, a glow in your heart, and your back to a great log fire, knowing that a feast of your choice is at your command. Go to your bed with a feeling that the world is a good place to be in, and anticipate another day of leisure and gracious living.

Fosters Smokehouse offers all this and more:
Golfing, Fishing, Walking, Climbing, Motoring, Thinking or just Sitting.